AF605227

Praise for *Pragmatic Philanthropy*

"We must create a civilization where we can realize the best of human potential. This book helps us to understand how this vision is being realized in Asia today."

—Muhammad Yunus, *Nobel Laureate and Founder, the Grameen Bank*

"In today's world, leaders must rely on partnerships that connect across business, government and civil society. In Asia, partnerships are in evident display. Ruth A. Shapiro tells us how they help address our shared problems in ways that create win-win solutions."

—Dominic Barton, *Managing Director, McKinsey & Company*

"Charity has had a long and noble history in Asia. It has not, however, been the study of much research or documentation. *Pragmatic Philanthropy* makes an important contribution to understanding the way in which social investment in Asia takes place."

—Victor K. Fung, *Group Chairman of the Fung Group*

"Kiva is working in 80 countries. While some aspects of our work are consistent throughout the world, we have learned that it is essential to have on the ground knowledge in each of the localities where we make loans available. We must have trustworthy local partners and be familiar with local laws and practices. Dr. Ruth A. Shapiro's insights come from decades of work in Asia. This book provides a very helpful view into the way philanthropy and other types of social investment gets done in the region."

—Premal Shah, *Co-Founder & President, Kiva*

"As every great social entrepreneur knows, and as the Skoll Foundation has learned from our work with them, context matters. What works in Bangladesh may not translate to Indonesia, and vice versa. Successful social investment depends upon local knowledge and uptake, as Ruth A. Shapiro demonstrates in this valuable volume. Here she shares insights gained from her work in Asia together with some of the world's most promising philanthropists. *Pragmatic Philanthropy: Asian Charity Explained* is essential reading for change-agents working across the Asian continent, and for those seeking to support them."

—Sally Osberg, *President and CEO, Skoll Foundation*

"We are beginning to see dramatic increases in interest and activity in philanthropy in China and throughout Asia. We also need to see a commensurate degree of research and understanding of the sector. This book is a worthwhile effort to help close the gap between interest and impact."

—Xiulan Zhang, *Professor and Former Founding Dean, School of Social Development and Public Policy, Beijing Normal University, China*

"Although non-profit corporations have been in existence in a legal sense since 1898, the Kobe earthquake of 1995, which was followed by other natural disasters, has been a wake-up call for Japan. We see the need for citizens to be active in addressing our shared concerns, whether they are helping vulnerable people or reconstructing a devastated area. Studies like the one carried out by the Centre for Asian Philanthropy and Society help us to learn valuable lessons about what works in taking on these roles."

—Tatsuo Ohta, *Chairman, The Japan Association of Charitable Organizations*

"This book exemplifies the reason that I agreed to go on the board of the Centre for Asian Philanthropy and Society—it provides world-class analysis to a field that is understudied and misunderstood. For too long, philanthropists have worked on the premise that the rigor and analysis they use in their businesses are not applicable to their charitable investments. The opposite is the case as these types of investments are more difficult to measure and can touch the lives of many. Dr. Ruth A. Shapiro's book helps us to understand the dynamic nature of the Asian philanthropic sector and make more informed choices about how we invest our time and our resources."

—Elizabeth Eder Zobel de Ayala, *Chairman Teach for the Philippines*

"More and more people are thinking about philanthropy in a more methodical, intelligent way. It is important to understand deeply the issues you are dealing with and support solutions that make the most impact. Grounded in research and evidence, this book helps us to see how this trend is accelerating across Asia."

—Jamshyd Godrej, *Chairman, Godrej and Boyce*

"Our own Trust Barometer shows that trust is in crisis around the world. Nonprofit organizations tend to be more trusted than governments and companies but even their numbers are going down. In Asia, this lack of trust has significant ramifications for philanthropy and the charitable sector. This book helps us to understand why trust is in such short supply, why this matters and what we can do about it."

—Richard Edelman, *Chief Executive Officer, Edelman*

"The Djarum Foundation's work is grounded in community help, tolerance and mutual assistance. These are values that are integral to who we are and are shared by many in Indonesia and throughout out Asia. *Pragmatic Philanthropy* explains how these values underpin programs and practices of helping each other in Asia."

—Victor Hartono, *Chairman, The Djarum Foundation*

Ruth A. Shapiro • Manisha Mirchandani
Heesu Jang

Pragmatic Philanthropy

Asian Charity Explained

palgrave
macmillan

Ruth A. Shapiro
CAPS, Hong Kong SAR, China

Manisha Mirchandani
CAPS, Hong Kong SAR, China

Heesu Jang
CAPS, Hong Kong SAR, China

ISBN 978-981-10-7118-8 ISBN 978-981-10-7119-5 (eBook)
https://doi.org/10.1007/978-981-10-7119-5

Library of Congress Control Number: 2017959588

Cover image © Icon Depot / Noun Project
Cover design by Samantha Johnson

Printed on acid-free paper

This Palgrave Macmillan imprint is published by Springer Nature
The registered company is Springer Nature Singapore Pte Ltd.
The registered company address is: 152 Beach Road, #21-01/04 Gateway East, Singapore 189721, Singapore

Dedicated to my father Jerry Shapiro who taught me to think big

Foreword

Today, we often hear of the differences between India and China. And while there are differences, there are also some striking similarities. Both countries have extraordinary histories, great and enduring philosophies and have arrived in the twenty-first century having rekindled their importance on the global stage. Both are moving past the damaging influences of colonial legacies as well as self-inflicted wounds while strengthening institutions and recognizing the benefits of being part of a globalized world.

As you read this book, you will see how much India and China have in common. In both countries, as in Asia more broadly, there is a tradition of taking care of one's family, one's clan, one's village. It is a tradition of charity where the more fortunate are expected to step up and help take care of those less so. There are expectations that when you are in need, the affluent will lend a helping hand. The richer helping the poorer has a long and storied history in our countries.

We also face similar challenges. Both countries have pulled millions out of poverty but both still have millions continuing to endure economic hardship. Both countries have created extraordinary wealth but wrestle with the challenge of extreme income inequality. Both countries are grappling with how to best organize local giving while at the same time dealing with the agendas of foreign donors. We are also trying to come to terms with China and India's international influence increasing at a time when the world order that has been in place since the end of World War II is in a state of flux.

There are other fundamental questions on the table. What does it mean to be part of a community? What are the responsibilities of those who have toward those who have not? And how does ancient ways of interacting with one another meld with modernity, technology and a cosmopolitan worldview? All of these big questions are embedded within the world of philanthropy.

This book looks at how these questions play out in the choices people make about how to help each other in eleven Asian economies. Culture and history surely play a role as does information and data. Throughout Asia, societies are evolving and new models of governance are being tested. Some of them will succeed and others will not but in the iterative process of moving forward, we will all continue to explore and experiment with the relationship between governments, companies and people.

Since the end of World War II, the United States has been the most dominant power in the world, with its soft power extending far beyond military and economic might. America has helped shape the way we think, the way we act, the way we dream and the way we treat one another. Much of this influence has been very positive and the world has welcomed the values prescribed in a Judeo-Christian set of principles. Now, at a time when India and China are once again becoming dominant world powers, the question is: what will be the influence of our soft power? This book, by casting a spotlight on Asian philanthropy, is coming at a pivotal moment in time.

We are pleased to be part of this conversation. Both of us have long embraced our fortunate ability to make contributions to improving people's lives and helping to progress societies. We see more and more of our peers coming to the realization that we have a role to play and we should do so with intention and with care. Post war modernity, globalism, education, and various reforms have accelerated job and wealth creation as well as philanthropy.

This book fills the important need of shining a light on the patterns of philanthropy and volunteer organizations in Asia today. It provides models and strategies of effective engagement as well as showcasing the changes now taking place.

We are pleased to be part of bringing this important book to the growing number of donors and philanthropists, government policymakers, non-profit leaders, teachers and students who may be drawn to social service and philanthropy and who can really use the information and insights contained here. For while we are living in extraordinary times, our humanity is what makes our world worth living in.

Chairman
Hang Lung Properties Ltd.
Hong Kong SAR, China

Ronnie C. Chan

Chairman
The Tata Trusts
Mumbai, India

Ratan Tata

Acknowledgments

This book is based on a 2-year project that could not have been pulled off without the support and teamwork of a great many people. This space is where I get to thank them.

Great thanks go to my co-authors Manisha Mirchandani and Heesu Jang. Manisha managed the case study project, edited a number of the cases, and wrote the one on the SEE Foundation herself. Her insights, her superb writing skills, the amazing way she befriends everyone and pulls them into our joint work will always be appreciated. Heesu jumped into the deep end with his chapter and pulled it off with great insight and aplomb. Mehvesh Mumtaz Ahmed stepped up as a great help with research when we most needed it. Sandy Collaco helped to make sure all appointments were made and kept in an always upbeat and positive manner.

I want to thank our board of trustees (Ronnie Chan, Daniel Tsai, Jamshyd Godrej, and Lizzie Zobel) and advisory board (Ratan Tata, Nazir Razak, Shin Dong Bin, and Vichit Suraphongchai), who agreed to take on this role due to a sincere desire to further our mission of improving the quality and quantity of private social investment in Asia. They also believed in me, for which I am incredibly grateful. I especially want to thank our Chairman Ronnie Chan. I have worked with Ronnie for 20 years, and it has been a very rewarding partnership. Together we built the Asia Business Council and now CAPS (Centre for Asian Philanthropy and Society). Ronnie is my boss (as he often reminds me!), my friend, and my collaborator, all enabling me to take on big goals and succeed with them.

We could not have done the case study project and built CAPS without our donors. There are very few independent research organizations in

Asia, and thus little familiarity with funding these types of endeavors. Our donors took the risk because they saw the opportunity and benefit that top-notch research could bring to the sector. Our donors to date are: The Aboitiz Foundation, Husodo Angkosubroto, Rahul Bajaj, Ronnie Chan and Hang Lung Properties Ltd., Fang Fang, Jamshyd Godrej and the Grodrej Trusts, Liu Chuanzhi, Azman Mokhtar and Yayasan Hasanah, Manny Pangilinan and the PLDT Foundation, Nazir Razak and the CIMB Foundation, Anthoni Salim, Stan Shih, Shin Dong Bin, Thapana Sirivadhanabhakdi and the Thai Beverage, SK Corporation, Vichit Suraphongchai and the Siam Commercial Bank Foundation, Tessie Sy-Coson and the BDO Foundation, George Tahija, Ratan Tata and the Tata Trusts, Daniel Tsai, Mary Ann Tsao, C.C. Tung, Zhang Lei and Hillhouse Capital, Susan Zhu, Jaime Zobel de Ayala and the Ayala Foundation and most recently, the Bill and Melinda Gates Foundation. Victor Fung of the Victor and William Fung Foundation not only underwrote a case study but also supported me both financially and spiritually in writing this book.

I would like to thank our many partners throughout Asia who helped write the case studies. These individuals and organizations worked with us to identify and write about exceptional nonprofit organizations and social enterprises whose stories and achievements help us to understand what it takes on the ground to bring about meaningful change. Among our partners, I would especially like to thank Tatsu Ohta at the Japan Association of Charitable Organizations, Jia Xijin and the Institute of Philanthropy at Tsinghua University, Wang Zhenyao and the China Philanthropy Research Institute, Jennifer Chen at Nanhua University, Huang Ping-der of the National Chengchi University, Danny Lam at Hong Kong University, Terence Yuen at the Chinese University of Hong Kong, Zhu Jiangang at the Sun Yat-sen University, Felix Tonog at Philippines Business for Social Progress, Carn Abella and her team at the Ramon Magsaysay Foundation, Kemal Soeryadja and his colleagues at Company-Community Partnerships for Health in Indonesia (CCPHI), Maria Radyati at Trisakti University, Professor Lam Swee Sum and her colleagues at the Asia Centre for Social Entrepreneurship and Philanthropy at the National University of Singapore, Madame Juree Vichit-Vadakan at the Center for Philanthropy and Civil Society at the Thai National Institute for Development Administration, Martin Tan at the Institute of Societal Leadership at Singapore Management University, Deval Sanghavi and his colleagues at Dasra, Tata Institute of Social Sciences, Kiran Pasricha at the Ananta Center, Lisa Dacanay and the Institute of Social Entrepreneurship in Asia, and Nini Daing and her colleagues at MyHarapan.

I would also like to extend my great appreciation and admiration for all the social delivery organizations (SDOs) and social enterprises we profiled in our case studies. The men and women who are involved with these organizations are the true heroes of this story. They toil day-in and day-out, often in very difficult circumstances for typically low pay to make our world a better place. Among this group, special thanks to Nellie Fong, Yao Li, Michael Chen, Rili Djohani, and Dr. Jemilah Mahmood.

I want to thank Sara Crowley-Vigneau at Palgrave Macmillan, who saw the promise of this book and answered every query with a way forward and great enthusiasm and support. My editor Dan Newman and copy editor John Zipperer provided sharp and insightful suggestions and knew when to add useful examples or cut unnecessary prose.

I would like to thank my daughters Shana and Zoe who have always cheered me on and given me the best reasons to spend my time working to address societal challenges. Lastly, I want to thank my best friend and husband Michael Gallagher, who has supported me in every way and put up with an absent wife so that I can fulfill my dream of creating the Centre for Asian Philanthropy and Society.

Founder and Chief Executive Ruth A. Shapiro
The Centre for Asian Philanthropy and Society
Hong Kong SAR, China

Contents

List of Authors

Heesu Jang is Research Associate for the Centre for Asian Philanthropy and Society. Prior to this, Heesu has worked for the United Nations High Commissioner for Refugees in Seoul, and for Bloomberg in Hong Kong. Heesu holds a Bachelor of Arts with Departmental Honors and Cum Laude in Political Science from the University of California, Los Angeles, where he focused on Chinese and Korean domestic politics and foreign policy. He has lived in Korea, China, and Hong Kong, and he is fluent in English, Korean, and Mandarin.

Manisha Mirchandani is an experienced researcher and author, who has written for the United Nations Development Programme, The Economist Group and The Economist Intelligence Unit (EIU). She has covered a wide range of topics on development and economic prosperity in Asia and was responsible for designing and executing bespoke research programmes for corporations, government organisations and multilateral institutions. She served as the project director at the Centre for Asian Philanthropy and Society in 2015–16. Manisha holds a BA from the University of Liverpool and an MSc from the London School of Economics.

Ruth A. Shapiro is the Founder and Chief Executive of the Centre for Asian Philanthropy and Society (CAPS). Ruth has spent her career focused on addressing social challenges in Asia. She founded the Asia Business Council and served as its Executive Director since its inception in 1997 until May 2007. She spent the early part of her professional career in the field of international development and held management positions at the

Academy for Educational Development, the Harvard Institute of International Development and Global Outlook. Ruth holds a doctorate from Stanford University and Master's Degrees from Harvard University and George Washington University. She completed her undergraduate work at the University of Michigan.

CHAPTER 1

Asian Philanthropy Explained

Ruth A. Shapiro

Asian philanthropy is not well understood. Although charity has come through individual and family efforts in the region for millennia, only in recent years has philanthropy developed as a widespread, systematic practice. It is growing and becoming increasingly important to society. Studies on the topic are rare—there are more than ten times as many books on American philanthropy as on Asian philanthropy—despite the evidence of a new approach to giving in Asia. Asian philanthropic ventures are not following the path of their Western counterparts, but rather are advancing along their own lines. These uncharted waters need maps.

This book aims to show how Asian philanthropy works. The traits of Asian philanthropy differ from similar practices in the West. These traits are visible across national lines, under many kinds of government, and in a variety of disciplines. They are adaptations to the unique environment in which Asian giving takes place.

What makes Asian philanthropy different, and why has it been so little studied? The most obvious answer is that until relatively recently, Asia has been poor. Given the region's remarkable growth in recent years, it is hard to remember that only in the last generation have significant numbers of Asians approached the common living standards of the West. Korean development was slow following the "temporary" conclusion of the

R.A. Shapiro
CAPS, Hong Kong SAR, China

R.A. Shapiro et al., *Pragmatic Philanthropy*,
https://doi.org/10.1007/978-981-10-7119-5_1

Korean War in 1953. It wasn't until 1978 that South Korea became a middle-income economy.[1] In India, almost a third of the population lives below the poverty line. Even China, which has moved more people out of extreme poverty in the past 30 years than any nation has done before, still struggles with its impoverished past; more than 200 million Chinese continue to live on less than $1.25 per day.[2]

When lifting itself out of poverty, Asia naturally focused on economic development first. Without much perceived wealth in a given nation, less attention went to sharing it. But that has changed dramatically in recent years. Singapore, which at the time of its independence in 1965 lacked adequate sanitation and housing, now has a per-capita income of $56,700, the third highest in the world. China now has more billionaires than the United States.[3]

It is difficult for those outside of Asia to see how rapid and transformative the growth in wealth has been. China went from having a per-capita income of $1100 in 1994 to $6300 in 2015. India went from $600 to $1800 in the same period. Indonesia's leap has been even greater, reducing the percentage of those living in poverty from 23.4 percent of the population in 1999 to 11.3 percent in 2014, an extraordinary achievement.[4]

While the average per-capita income in many Asian countries might still not be high, the numbers reflect much more disposable income in general. Many people and many nations in Asia have moved firmly into middle-income status, and within them, there are high earners with incomes far above the mean.

There are many analyses of what Asian countries did right in order to bring about this dramatic shift. One of the most influential of these was *The East Asian Miracle*, published by the World Bank in 1993, which explained the rise in income of eight Asian economies from 1965 to 1990 due to two fundamentally important policies and programs: (1) sound fiscal policies creating overall macroeconomic stability, and (2) the development of human capital through the provision of universal primary education.[5]

It makes sense that the poor are not philanthropists, nor is there a widespread tendency to create nonprofit organizations to help others when one is worried about food, shelter, and health care. Only with the availability of disposable income can philanthropy rise, alongside the creation of social delivery organizations (SDOs). Until recently, most philanthropy in Asia came from Western foundations and through development assistance. This is changing. Asia is the most dynamic and fast-growing economic region in the world, and philanthropy is rising as the economies grow.

A second reason for the sparse track record of Asian philanthropy is a dearth of information. Until now, Asia-based universities have focused their attention on other issues. Given the need to concentrate on economic development, this is not surprising. It is also not surprising that the situation is changing rapidly. University departments looking at philanthropy and civil society have come into existence in the past few years. In some of the region's top universities, departments dedicated to the study of philanthropy and/or nonprofit management are emblematic of this trend. The National University of Singapore (NUS) created a program in 2011, Hong Kong University in 2014, and Tsinghua University in Beijing in 2015.

The "Asian Way"

To get an accurate picture of the charitable sector in any region, it helps to understand how society views philanthropy and social delivery organizations. The cultural propensity to give and receive charitable donations varies not only by place but also over time. In Chapter 2, we provide the historical overview by country. Here, we can note that while there is great variation throughout Asia, there is one clear strand throughout much of Asian history: the tendency to give first and foremost to family and clan.

Even in the West, philanthropists give partly out of self-interest. Certain wealthy donors like to have their gifts noted for the public, or even to have new buildings and developments named after them. Some gifts are made partly for tax purposes. Asian donors value these things, too, but they go a step further. In making philanthropic donations, Asians commonly donate as a function of personal contacts as well as to organizations that expand their business networks. Thus, donations typically enhance personal and business relationships while also providing support to some important work.

Support for such efforts is influenced by each nation's legal and regulatory environment, which in turn stems from historical precedent. Laws encouraging or discouraging the giving and receiving of philanthropic donations change with time. In Asia, such laws are in flux to a greater degree than in the West. There is widespread ambiguity and confusion about what the sector can do. There are two major reasons for this.

One reason is that in Asia, people are still shaping their views about who is responsible for supporting the social sector. Isn't government supposed to be responsible for providing education, health care, jobs, and livelihood? Isn't government supposed to insure the health, well-being, safety, and security of its citizens? In short, of course, the answer is yes. But organizations and individuals can also help provide a social good. In a modern world, with decentralized information and ample digital tools, government might no longer be best suited to delivering all services and goods deemed necessary for the social contract. In the wake of the Asian and global financial crises, governments might also not be ideally positioned to promote all programs for the general good. Public and private outreach can work in tandem to keep a stronger social contract.

The second reason is that, in Asia, there is not widespread consensus on the value proposition of civil society and the role of private citizens. For a Western reader, this question may seem surprising as the establishment of nonprofit organizations, of think tanks, of private philanthropy does not, in the overwhelming majority of cases, pose any existential risk to the government. In a robust democratic society, multiple opinions, analyses, activities, and outcomes are not only tolerated but also lauded. In the West, a paramount role of civil society is to check the power of the government and of the private sector. Civil society is an integral component of a pluralist system. Even the term *civil society* is often used to mean the collective voices of the people as *opposed* to government and business. In Asia, many see democracy as a messy process with unclear benefits. In fact, democratic participation isn't as widely valued as economic growth, stability, and other measures of societal progress. In Asia, the term *civic engagement* might be more accurate than civil society.

If this sounds like modern China, such values are indeed in place. But questions about the costs of democracy come up in many places, with many people. Even in countries with strong democratic histories such as India and the Philippines, there is more than a little frustration expressed about the difficult nature of democratic decision-making processes and the role of civic actors further complicating the process. This frustration can help to explain why in both countries, "strong men" Narendra Modi and Rodrigo Duterte were recently elected as the heads of state. In countries with more authoritarian regimes, the question of what role private actors play in delivering a social good becomes a front-burner issue. In fact, in many Asian countries today, including India, China, Malaysia, Indonesia, and the Philippines, new laws and regulations for the creation and conduct of philanthropic and social delivery organizations are being proposed and enacted, some promoting the practice and others restricting it.

When governments implement restrictions, they are frequently aimed at advocacy groups. When Westerners read about governments limiting the reach of non-governmental organizations in Asia, they are typically reading about groups endeavoring to change the status quo in ways broader than addressing the specific societal challenge. A group seeking to improve eye care in rural China or Indonesia may well be accepted, but one aiming to strengthen citizen legal representation may not.

Though the discussion about the role that advocacy groups play in society is a worthwhile one, it is not the point of our study and of this book. We are confining our analysis to social delivery organizations (SDOs), those aiming to provide social benefits within the given political framework of each nation, and even among those, to groups working in areas associated with basic human needs such as education, health, poverty alleviation, and the environment. Advocacy organizations working in areas such as human rights, legal reform, and labor issues do important work, but it is also necessary to clarify the differences between these types of efforts and those that seek to address challenges lower on Maslow's hierarchy, which places food, shelter, and health among our basic needs.

The distinction between SDOs and advocacy organizations can be difficult to ascertain. Many SDOs also advocate for regulatory change around a specific set of issues. As we will see later in the book, a number of the organizations we studied were encouraged to provide input to the government. Bainian Vocational Services, for example, worked with the government to change the scope and availability of vocational training opportunities for children of migrant workers and the rural poor. Eden Social Welfare Foundation pushed government to create greater access for the disabled in Taiwan, and the Magic Bus was instrumental in getting the Indian government to change educational policies and programs around sports and athletic programs.

But when we talk about advocacy organizations and those that are encountering resistance in Asia, we are specifically referring to those organizations that combine two elements: (1) they do not have intervention programs and spend 100 percent of their time and financial resources on policy change; and (2) these changes are perceived by government as antagonistic rather than complementary. Throughout Asia, the largest donations to these types of organizations come from outside the region. For this reason, states such as India and China are reassessing the way that foreign funding comes into the country and the types of organizations it supports. Currently, in many countries around the world, the degrees of freedom for foreign-funded advocacy organizations are shrinking. This book does not make a judgment about these changes, but merely attempts to describe the phenomena and the possible ramifications on local philanthropy and SDOs.

In the chapter on changing government policies we will explain in greater detail why this is the case, but the simple answer is that within the Asian context, there is far less appetite to fund efforts that publicly criticize government. Although there has not been perfect harmony between the views of government and private businesses or individuals, they have often worked in tandem on aligned agendas related to economic growth. While that is true to an extent in other parts of the world, we will see throughout this book that there are important differences between Western civil society and Asian civic engagement.

What are the roles of philanthropic and non-governmental, SDOs in Asia?

The primary role is to help others in need because it is possible to do so. Helping others is an integral tenet of what it means to be human and has been promoted through the ages in civilizations around the world. The premise and intent are clear. More difficult to determine are the differences in definition and motivation between charity and philanthropy. Are they alike? Charity is the act of giving money, food, or other kinds of help to people who are poor, sick, or need other types of help. Philanthropy is an active effort to promote human welfare. In other words, philanthropy is a formalized and systematic process of being charitable. This book deals with organizations and organized, systematic approaches to helping those in need.

The context for such efforts necessarily includes government. Individual and corporate philanthropy is on the rise, but it is a small amount compared to public spending. In the United States, with the largest and most active philanthropic sector in the world, American foundations together spent about $375 billion on all programs and sectors, compared to $3.8 trillion in federal spending for 2015. Of that federal money, more than $1 trillion went to health and human services. Private donations remain much smaller. This means that even in the United States, with the largest and most robust philanthropic organizations, private funds equal only a small fraction of the financial resources spent by the government.

As a result, one effective use of philanthropic investment is in areas not ordinarily underwritten by government. This thinking results in pilot projects, basic research, riskier ventures in a variety of sectors, and much of the support for arts and humanities.

Our research shows that in Asia, there is an implicit social contract at work. As will be described in greater detail later in the book, Asian philanthropy tends not to go to advocacy organizations, but is in line with and often in partnership with governmental objectives. Though societal forces are driving a revision of this contract in many places, our study shows fundamental differences in how philanthropy and nonprofit organizations work alongside and with governments in the region. Much of this can be understood by looking back at the concept of the "Asian way."

The concept of Asian values or the term *Asian way* came into popular use under Lee Kwan Yew of Singapore and Malaysia's Mahathir Mohamad in the 1990s. The term is used to describe a cultural predisposition toward harmony and collectivism rather than individualism. These preferences also entail greater acceptance of benevolent authoritarian regimes, those offering greater material wealth and a rule-based, but harmonious, society.

The term *Asian way* has been both embraced and condemned. The notion that there is a difference in how societies in Asia are structured and evolve, compared to their Western counterparts, has been disputed for years. Many scholars predicted that Asia would be like the West once given enough time as many Western nations had more similar conditions a generation or two ago. Indeed, the term *Asian way* has been out of favor for years, and the region's heterogeneity means the concept is probably too grand and sweeping to cast much light on its modern connotations. But as seems clear from our study, there is some truth to elements of an Asian way, an implicit social contract with government and the deeply rooted tendency to seek harmony.

With this concept, Lee and Mahathir strove to counter the view that Asia is remarkably diverse by saying that within their own multiethnic countries, there are common traits and behaviors that allow for a more collectivist mindset and agenda. It's a bold aim. How can one make statements about a region that covers 50 countries and more than 4.5 billion people? While it would be ridiculous to say that Asia is homogeneous, one can say that there are certain cultural tendencies and behaviors that can be seen across many countries, especially those in East, Southeast, and to a certain extent South Asia. Certain concepts that have emerged from our research—community, cooperation, collaboration—underpin societies across the region, and they provide useful hooks on which to place understanding about Asian philanthropy.

With the above points in mind, a number of Asian governments have begun to come to terms with the existence and benefits of encouraging private philanthropy and the organizations that receive these funds. This is not to say that there are not also rules as to how, when, and where the funds and their beneficiary organizations are to work.

The effect of these rules can easily be seen in Singapore, one of the leaders in recognizing the positive role of citizen engagement in the social sector. Since 2009, qualifying donations have been granted a 250 percent tax deduction including a period of time when it went up to 300%. Not surprisingly, charitable contributions have gone up significantly; 30 percent since the law took effect.[6] According to many donors, this move by the government was important not only because of the tax benefit, especially as the tax rate in Singapore is low, but also because it signals to the public that the government endorses this kind of giving. Such signals carry tremendous weight in other Asian nations as well. In Singapore's case, as in a number of other Asian countries, it is important to understand that only those organizations aligned with government policies are able to get the appropriate accreditations to qualify for receiving these donations.

Elsewhere in Asia, government policy has been less targetted. In India and China, there has been a seemingly mixed set of policies. On the one hand, both governments have endorsed rules to encourage increased giving, but on the other, they have enacted constraints on existing organizations and philanthropies. The policies result from wariness of advocacy groups alongside an increasingly positive view of less controversial philanthropy flowing to social delivery organizations.

India is the first country in the world to require the top companies by market share to provide 2 percent of their after-tax profits to corporate social responsibility activities. As with Singapore, the funds need to go to accredited organizations or government projects, which include programs to eradicate hunger, boost education, improve environmental practices, and to support the prime minister's relief fund. A company can implement these activities on its own, through its own nonprofit foundation, or through independently registered nonprofit organizations that have a record of at least three years in similar activities. Not surprisingly, the law has spurred a boom in the establishment of NGOs in India—as well as in the number of consultants to advise companies on how to spend the funds.

At the same time, India has put foreign organizations, such as the Ford Foundation, under increased scrutiny. Since coming into office, Prime Minister Narendra Modi has linked foreign funding received by some NGOs to the ongoing unrest in the country, and he has emphasized the importance of more tightly regulating the sector.[7] In April 2017, the Indian government revoked the licenses of nearly 9000 nonprofit organizations that had received donations from the West. This move was seen as retaliation—along with restrictions placed on the activities and funds of

Greenpeace and the Ford Foundation—against groups that had taken anti-Modi stances. At first blush, the two policies of encouraging corporate giving and clamping down on foreign funding for NGOs seem schizophrenic. The reality is more nuanced. The Modi government encourages programs in line with its own development and social agenda. Whether or not it is fair, it has a utilitarian logic. Most organizations went along with the directive. One international foundation spokesperson said, "We believe that our role is to provide catalytic support in areas that are aligned with the priorities of the government of India."

In China, the government has also been warming to the constructive possibilities of philanthropy and SDOs. That may be due to recognition of their benefits, or because the state realizes it cannot, alone, address the impending needs of an aging, more demanding populace. In either case, support of SDOs has received official endorsement. Chapter 39 of the 5-year plan (2011–2015) states that it seeks to "Strengthen the supervision and management of social organizations including cultivation, development, management and supervision of social organizations, promoting their healthy and orderly development…reflecting appeals of the citizenry and standardizing behavior."

China is working out the extent to which NGOs can have latitude in crafting and implementing their own solutions. The recently enacted charity law followed 11 years of consultation and discussion with many in the sector worried it would concentrate primarily at curtailing foreign-funded advocacy organizations, those posing a risk to its "ideological security."[8] That does not appear to be its sole intent: the law addresses ways of making charitable donations and the use of funds more transparent and accountable, decreasing the likelihood of fraud. But the law does regulate the types of donations a tax-exempt organization can receive and how and how quickly the funds must be spent. The law also calls for local government agencies to get more involved in overseeing nonprofits, and it is unclear how supportive or open-minded local officials will be. Time will tell if the law will make civic engagement easier and more effective, or not.

Conflicting attitudes toward NGOs are apparent in other ways. In February of 2016, President Xi Jinping called on wealthy Chinese to help the poor through philanthropy—fitting timing when many high-net-worth individuals are seeking purpose with their wealth. Yet around the same time, Beijing began to modify the law allowing foreign nonprofit organizations to operate in China. The adjustment seemed to be aimed primarily at those organizations engaged in advocacy work. As Ma Jun, founder of the Institute of Public and Environmental Affairs (IPE) explains, "Nonprofit organizations in China must recognize the reality of our national condition."[9] Social work, in line with government policy, is encouraged. Advocacy work is more narrowly tolerated, if at all.

The trend is clear. Some governments in Asia will allow and even encourage increased activity from philanthropic and social delivery organizations, as long as their work suits the government's own agenda.

A "Trust Deficit"

Legal fluctuations have been an important factor contributing to a widespread "trust deficit" among SDOs, donors, government, and the public at large. SDOs are not viewed with the same confidence they inspire in the West, and many individuals curtail their giving as a result. In fact, in our interviews with dozens of high-net-worth individuals around Asia, lack of trust in local organizations was the number-one reason cited for the low degree of giving to Asia-based organizations.

Murky and fluctuating regulations and tax policies signal to the public that government is unsure about philanthropy and social delivery organizations. It is not surprising that with the Singaporean tax subsidy, philanthropic giving went up considerably. There are other reasons for the trust deficit, however.

The most damaging influence on public trust in SDOs has been the wide, varied, and highly public scandals that have affected the sector, most especially those that include fraud and the misuse of donated funds. Most Asian nations have had recent experiences with these types of public scandals causing quite a stir in their home economies. The growing role of social media and its freer flow of information has expanded awareness of many such incidents. In 2011, a woman claiming to be an employee of the Red Cross in China posted a picture of herself with her new Maserati, raising popular fury. The Red Cross denied that she was an employee, but an official investigation was never undertaken, and the public remained suspicious that funds had been misused.

In any case, official donations dropped more than 80 percent as a result. Even squeaky-clean Singapore had a very public scandal, when one of the nation's largest charities, the National Kidney Foundation, was found to have misappropriated funds in 2005.

Lack of transparency and disclosure by SDOs has not eased such wariness. In most Asian countries, SDOs are not required to be transparent.

In Korea, most large nonprofit organizations list some financial information on their websites; but because they are overseen by different ministries, each of which has different reporting requirements, the type and quality of the information they provide is varied and weak. In India, accountability expectations are low, and only 600 NGOs out of an estimated 500,000 have so far subscribed to the high standards of the Credibility Alliance, a watchdog aiming to improve trust through better governance.

In China, work by the China Foundation Center (CFC) has helped foundations become increasingly transparent. Because many foundations in China are actually operating organizations, the work of the CFC covers a number of SDOs. Those organizations choosing to be transparent, by providing their annual reports for public viewing and through other means, tend to find it easier to raise necessary funds. CFC now has data on 4000 foundations.

Social delivery organizations are often not required to be transparent, and many lack the expertise and skills to provide this information even if they want to. Any such inability adds to the perception of charities as lacking in skill, talent, and effectiveness. Some presume they need not learn such skills beyond showing cost savings. That perception is changing as impact and effectiveness become more important than measures of overhead and costs. The skill set of SDOs is also improving as more people choose to go into public service either out of college or as an "encore" career. Business engagement, especially through corporate social responsibility programs, is also improving the professional skills and understanding of SDO staff members. In Chapter 7 we will explore various ways that business is playing a role in influencing the sector and expectations for the SDO sector.

Much of this is new. University programs in this sector have not been around long, and they are still not widespread. Furthermore, there are few supplemental training programs outside of university. SDO staff might have hearts of gold, but they often have not been shown how to establish solid accounting systems, to evaluate their impact, or to tell stories of their programs in a professional manner.

Lastly, a factor that increases distrust is the question about how to define an NGO or a nonprofit organization. Currently, there is no Asian nation that legally differentiates advocacy organizations from social delivery organizations. This reality, coupled with a lack of transparency, means that it is often unclear what a given group aims to do and how well it will be tolerated. Although many SDOs do have an advocacy component to them, it might be useful to designate those with the sole aim of policy change from those that are carrying out programmatic initiatives.

An Empirical Analysis

So what makes a successful SDO? What makes an effective philanthropist, and what constitutes good philanthropic practices?

With the increasing number of philanthropists in Asia, some funders and consultants have stepped up to offer guidance as they determine what and how they will fund, though the number of organizations in this space remains very small compared to the West. The Centre for Asian Philanthropy and Society (CAPS) is one of the few Asia-based organizations doing work in this space. We understand that just as in business, the most effective strategies may vary with the location. To determine which approaches worked best, we began our substantive, empirically based research on effective practices within the Asian context.

Asian economies have done very well in the past couple of decades, creating a growing middle- and high-income class in the region. Disposable income translates to the purchase of consumer goods such as phones, televisions, and cars, but it also means that many more have the ability to think about giving back to their communities, about addressing societal inequalities, and about improving education, health care, and the environment, among other issues. In Asia, the result is an increase in the number of SDOs, and also a rise in the activity of philanthropists.

Throughout this book, we will use the term *social delivery organization* (SDO). As will be explained in a subsequent chapter, the term *NGO* (nongovernmental organization) is not appropriate as many of these organizations are connected to the government. *Nonprofit organization* is also not appropriate given the rise of social enterprises and other profit-making income streams.

Asian philanthropists are making news. Take, for example, Ronnie Chan, CAPS' Hong Kong-based chairman. Mr. Chan and his brother Gerald donated US$350 million to Harvard University in 2015, at that time the largest contribution in Harvard's history. Or look at Azim Premji, who put US$2 billion into his foundation for innovative improvements to India's 1.3 million government-run schools. More and more individuals are joining this nascent field to deploy growing funds, create more programs, and bring positive changes to the quality of people's lives.

To get a clear view of what is happening on the ground in Asia regarding philanthropy and SDOs, CAPS has carried out 30 case studies and other research with 42 partners in 11 economies. Each of the case studies is available on our website (www.caps.org/research). This book shares our findings across the case studies and answers the following questions:

- Is there an "Asian" way of doing good? If there is, why so, and what are the implications?
- What is the Asian philanthropy and social delivery ecosystem, and how has it evolved?
- What are the characteristics and strategies of successful Asian SDOs?
- Why is it important to distinguish between SDOs and other types of nonprofit organizations?
- What are trends of Asian philanthropists and why?
- What are shared challenges for the region?
- What can donors, SDOs, policymakers, and the public at large do to enable the social sector to thrive and contribute to improving the lives of people throughout the region?

Why Case Studies?

We needed to understand if there are important differences in how ideas are formulated, coalitions built, and work undertaken in Asia. To do so, we sought out successful organizations to analyze the ingredients that enabled their success. We also studied their funders and other philanthropists in the region to see if there are shared characteristics involved with their giving.

Subjects of the case studies as well as our partners in this project vary in type. Some are nonprofit organizations. Others are quasi-governmental groups, and yet others are corporate foundations. Several combine business enterprise with social good. Landwasher, a for-profit firm, has found a low-energy way to provide sanitation systems in China. The Eden Social Welfare Foundation in Taiwan provides services and generates 25 percent of its income from businesses involving the disabled. Our studies on other hybrids of profit/nonprofit and public/private partnerships help us see the different roles they play in their respective contexts.

Each of our chosen groups aligns with the priorities of the Sustainable Development Goals, a set of 17 global benchmark issues broadly seen as essential. We focused on four categories: education, health, poverty alleviation, and the environment. Another criterion was that each be free from scandal, not a simple requirement when many groups are stronger on passion and commitment than on record keeping and accounting. We wanted organizations with impeccable credentials.

All are local groups, not local branches affiliated with international organizations. Some of our donors questioned this criterion, as they have close relationships with global organizations. But international nonprofits come with established tool kits; they have governance systems, know how to fundraise, and conduct measurement and evaluation. We wanted to know how local conditions influenced all of those we studied from the start. We felt so strongly about this that we had to let one donor to walk away when she would not support this focus to our learning—a tough decision for a new organization operating on a shoestring!

Finally, we wanted to find organizations that offered an opportunity to learn something new—those that had introduced an innovation, or scaled their impact, or had evolved in a meaningful way. We wanted each case study to offer useful lessons.

The case studies have allowed us to identify characteristics and strategies of successful Asia-based SDOs. Through them, we have been able to interact with a range of Asian philanthropists and business leaders to gain deeper awareness about what motivates them in their giving. These benefits together allow us to paint a picture of the state of the field today.

Notes

1. According to the World Bank, Korea reached a per capita income of \$1026~\$4035, making it a lower middle-income country (in today's dollars). World Development Indicators| World DataBank. The World Bank: World Development Indicators, Retrieved from [http://databank.worldbank.org/data/reports.aspx?source=world-development-indicators] n.d. Web. 12 Aug.
2. Frank, Robert. "China Has More Billionaires than the U.S." CNBC. February 24,2016.https://www.cnbc.com/2016/02/24/china-has-more-billionaires-than-us-report.html
3. Chun Han Wong. "More than 82 Million Chinese Live on Less than \$1 a Day." *The Wall Street Journal.* October 15, 2014. https://blogs.wsj.com/chinarealtime/2014/10/15/more-than-82-million-chinese-live-on-less-than-1-a-day/
4. The World Bank. India State Briefs and Indonesia State Briefs, "India: Poverty Profile," and Indonesia: Poverty Profile: May 26, 2016.

5. Birdsall, Nancy M.; Campos, Jose Edgardo L.; Kim, Chang-Shik; Corden, W. Max; MacDonald, Lawrence [editor]; Pack, Howard; Page, John; Sabor, Richard; Stiglitz, Joseph E. *The East Asian Miracle: Economic Growth and Public Policy*, The World Bank, Washington, DC. September 26, 1993. The eight economies studied are those of Hong Kong, Indonesia, Japan, Malaysia, Korea, Singapore, Taiwan, and
6. Chew, Hui Min. "Singapore Budget 2015: Tax Deduction of 300 Percent the Amount Donated in Jubilee Year." February 23, 2015. http://www.straitstimes.com/singapore/singapore-budget-2015-tax-deduction-of-300-per-cent-the-amount-donated-in-jubilee-year. AccessedApril 10, 2016.
7. Manku, Moyna. "Government NGO Distrust Deepening." *The Mint*. February 21, 2016. http://www.livemint.com/Politics/JguEQTdy3IhtfqxLjC8diL/GovernmentNGO-distrust-deepening.html. Accessed April 6, 2016.
8. Wong, Edward. "Chinese Security Laws Elevate the Party and Stifle Dissent." *The New York Times*. May 29, 2015. https://www.nytimes.com/2015/05/30/world/asia/chinese-national-security-law-aims-to-defend-party-grip-on-power.html?mcubz=0. Accessed April 6, 2016.
9. Shapiro, Ruth A. 真正的问题解决者:社会企业如何用创新改变世界. Cheers Publishing Company, Beijing, 2015.

CHAPTER 2

Old Money—The History of Giving in Asia

Heesu Jang

In 2010, Warren Buffett and Bill Gates visited China to convince their Chinese millionaire and billionaire counterparts to commit to giving large portions of their wealth to charity. During this time, the Western media's portrayal of the philanthropic landscape in China, such as that by The Associated Press, was that it was "relatively immature." Journals readily noted that while China's GDP has recently come to reach half of America's, the United States philanthropic market was still 21 times larger.[1]

Like China, other Asian economies are frequently subject to similar news coverage whenever prominent Western businessmen pay visits to promote philanthropy throughout the region. While it celebrates its Gates, Ford, Carnegie, and Rockefeller families as generous and selfless champions of philanthropy, it calls for greater action from Asia as a whole.

Admittedly, Asia is outnumbered, outweighed, and outscored by the West on most fronts within the charitable sector. The West in general boasts more philanthropists, more individual donors, and more organizations, not to mention the sheer amount and scope of donations. Nevertheless, contrary to the claims of the media, the clear superiority of the West in these measures does not dictate Asia's capacity for doing good.

To better make sense of this apples-to-oranges comparison between Asian and Western philanthropy, one must first revisit the difference and

H. Jang
CAPS, Hong Kong SAR, China

R.A. Shapiro et al., *Pragmatic Philanthropy*,
https://doi.org/10.1007/978-981-10-7119-5_2

the relationship between charity and philanthropy defined by the first chapter of this book: philanthropy is a formalized and systematic process of doing good, while charity is the act of doing good itself. That is, even though philanthropy in Asia may be "relatively immature" due to the continent's rather late economic growth and exposure to the concept, history tells us Asians, too, know how to be charitable and generous.

Four key historical experiences are shared by most, if not all, Asian economies. First, Asians emphasize caring for the well-being of fellow community members, from family to locality. Second, religions significantly influence the giving and helping behaviors and patterns of Asian countries and peoples, with many religious institutions even going so far as to deliver social services to the people. Third, modern civil society in most Asian countries flourished as either a challenging force against, or as a direct result of, twentieth-century colonialism. Finally, the public image and personality of modern civil society in Asia has been shaped by past interactions and experiences with powerful central governments. This chapter will explore in greater detail these themes of community, faith, colonialism, and authoritarianism for each of the 11 Asian economies, to demonstrate how Asia's long history of generosity and charity will help pave way for a philanthropic tomorrow.

India

Socioeconomic incongruities coexist in India. Considered one of the leading developing countries in terms of annual GDP growth, India still suffers from nationwide poverty. One in five Indians is poor, and an estimated 270 million citizens live below the poverty line.[2] Basic sanitation, health care, education, and other social services are not readily available to much of the local population.

Accompanying some of these alarming challenges are promising trends. India is renowned for its advanced information technology sector, as well as for housing major homegrown multinational corporations across various industries. It boasts more than 100 billionaires, consistently ranking India in the top five with the likes of the United States, China, and Germany.[3] And it is the largest democracy in the world.

India's philanthropy reflects such contrasts. With socioeconomic hardships alongside a dynamic marketplace full of new wealth, the gap for Indian charity and philanthropy to tap into is glaringly apparent.

Preceding this present-day environment favorable for charitable individuals and institutions is a rich track record of giving—both informal and formal—that predated even the pioneers in American philanthropic history.

From the late nineteenth century to the early twentieth century, India for the first time witnessed the establishment of modern foundations by prominent members of the private sector, including the J. N. Tata Endowment Scheme (1892) and the N. M. Wadia Foundation (1909).[4]

India also possesses a deeply ingrained culture of informal giving.[5] Providing financial and non-financial support to one's immediate family and community (caste, village, or other extended social groups) is common. This culture resonates across the country today: 24 percent of donors reported having given money to their friends, neighbors, and colleagues, while 53 percent of donors indicated that an unreturned loan to a family relative is a donation.[6] Families also provided various social services to their domestic helpers in addition to their paid salary. Clothing and food were common donations, along with financial contributions to their health care and their children's education.

Finally, donating for religious purposes has historically been a major part of Indian giving. In fact, charitable religious endowments and trusts came before modern philanthropic institutions. Donations frequently went to Islamic endowments specifically for charitable purposes, known as *waqfs*, and to trusts like the Tirumala Tirupati Devasthanams that managed Hindu temples and provided social services such as schools and hospitals. India's organic institutionalization of philanthropy and long culture of family, community, and religious giving attest to the country's preexisting familiarity with and maturity in doing good.

This homegrown charity and philanthropy reflects India's strong faith-based textual roots to its generous culture. Hinduism—the most widespread religion in India today—Buddhism and Islam all contribute to Indians' inclination to do good. The concepts of *zakat* (almsgiving) and *sadaqaat* (voluntary offerings) in Islam and of *bhiksha* (food given as alms) and avoiding bad *karma* in Buddhism particularly pertain to giving.[7]

In Hinduism, many ancient Sanskrit texts are comprised of extremely detailed stipulations about charity and philanthropy.[8] That is, beyond simply encouraging benevolent actions, these sources spell out the who, what, when, why, and how of *daana* (giving) and *seva* (service). Kings were also required by the epic of Mahabharata to share their wealth with the people and not use it for their own pleasure. Sanskrit books even imply a hierarchy, as in the Laws of Manu, in which food, required by all beings for their survival, emerges as the best in worth over gold, silver, salt, and so on. A benefactor's attitude had to be genuine and passionate; certain traits were also expected of the beneficiary. In other words, giving merely for the sake of giving is insufficient, necessitating benefactors to check multiple boxes to give, strategically and efficiently.

Still, India has not been immune to external influence on its charitable and philanthropic sector. Industrialization during the British Raj era increased both the size and the scope of philanthropy in India.[9] With a modernized economy, the overall wealth of businesses exceeded an unprecedented amount, resulting in a bigger surplus for public welfare. At the same time, industrialization helped expand the market coverage of businesses and allowed them to operate beyond the regional confines of their respective headquarter cities, which in turn scaled up the scope of the private sector's philanthropic activities. Many domestic philanthropic foundations reflect India's inherent culture and history of goodwill, but they grew against the backdrop of industrialization that occurred under British colonial rule.

India's government played an important role. As early as 1860, India legally recognized the existence of nonprofit groups via the British Raj Societies Registration Act, granting the status of a "society" to a group of seven or more people in any literary, scientific, or charitable association.[10] Numerous nonprofit organizations and philanthropic foundations arose as a result, and this piece of legislation still applies to NGOs today.[11]

The legacy of the colonial era also shaped philanthropic thought. As many donors concluded that British dominance grew from advanced science and technology, philanthropists changed their giving priorities, funneling more money into relevant endeavors, as well as into projects of social reform.[12] More money was funneled into secular purposes, such as social reform and cultural revivalism projects. In the end, with Mahatma Gandhi's return to India in 1916, this particular evolution of Indian philanthropy culminated in a mobilized Indian civil society's involvement in the independence movement.

Gandhi's return in 1916 shifted the course of India's development plan to economic self-sufficiency. As part of this quest for self-sufficiency, voluntary action at the local village level became pivotal in the drive to tackle widespread poverty.[13] As a result, the number of village-oriented community organizations proliferated.[14] Gandhi's theory of trusteeship inspired many wealthy individuals at the time to donate money and resources for the good of the greater community, whether it would be for the independence movement or for the delivery of social services.[15] In so doing, Gandhi utilized many of the Hindu concepts relevant to charity and philanthropy in a way that transcended the terms' original definitions to bring about greater change in line with his goals.[16] He worked to transform the primary motive behind doing good from acquiring merit as a religious obligation to wholeheartedly wanting to contribute to the general welfare of all, stating, "You should regard yourself as the trustees and servants of the poor. Your commerce must be regulated for the benefit of the toiling millions and you must be satisfied with earning an honest penny."[17]

Gandhi also said, "Earn your crores by all means. But understand that your wealth is not yours; it belongs to the people. Take what you require for your legitimate needs, and use the remainder for society."[18] The Birla and Bajaj families were notably affected by the principles and theories of Gandhi and donated millions of rupees for causes that he promoted.[19]

Post-independence India (1948–1980s) further encouraged philanthropy. The socialist, interventionist government focused on social welfare and economic development, with a heavy dose of central planning.[20,21] The private sector supported the government's developmental agenda, and India experienced a dramatic increase in the number of private trusts and foundations.[22] The government, in turn, encouraged citizens' participation in social welfare programs, but some argue that the state's dominant role actually imposed limitations on the nonprofit sector, so that it was only the confrontational response to inefficient government that led to the burgeoning of the nonprofit sector in India.[23] Be that as it may, the outcome of growth in both philanthropy and charity in India is unquestionable.

Today, the charitable and philanthropic sector of India is one of the most vibrant in the world. Individual giving in India is a global outlier, trumping the rest of the world at its level of GDP per capita.[24] More than 2 million NGOs are reported to be active in the country, while the numbers of philanthropists and potential philanthropists in millionaires and billionaires are increasing every year.[25,26] The Companies Act of 2013 and its 2-percent corporate social responsibility spending requirement has had a huge impact, as will be seen in greater detail in a later chapter of this book. But the socioeconomic shortcomings, discussed in the beginning of this section, persist to plague the country, making the role of charity and philanthropy all the more imperative for the future trajectory of India.

Philippines

In the Philippines, we see the impact of all four themes: community, faith, colonialism, and authoritarianism. The Filipino lexicon reflects its deep cultural roots in traditions of *pakikipagkapwa*, a sense of shared community and *kapwa*, compassion. To this day, Catholicism plays a crucial role both in spiritually encouraging charity, as well as in directly providing basic social services to those in need. Two colonial regimes—Spanish and American—helped establish the initial infrastructure needed for its now vibrant civil society and philanthropic community, while the Marcos dictatorship cracked down heavily on advocacy groups, ultimately triggering a fierce counteraction from an extremely well-mobilized nonprofit sector.

In pre-colonial times, informal mechanisms of mutual self-help volunteerism prevailed throughout the country at the village level. Volunteers often helped with construction of public infrastructure projects such as churches, schoolhouses, streets, plazas, and cemeteries.[27] In fact, this domestically bred practice of *bayanihan* (assuming another's burdens) was more commonplace than religious associations exported by Catholicism and Spanish colonialism.[28] This unique history of alleviating fellow community members' hardships demonstrates the Filipinos' deeply ingrained fondness for community welfare, manifested in both the language and village-level volunteerism.

Under Spanish colonialism, the Philippines began to see for the first time the establishment of formal charitable organizations. Public goods institutions set up by the Roman Catholic Church left behind a significant legacy of introducing institutionalized social delivery organizations (SDOs), alongside individual philanthropic giving to the Church.[29] With its funds, the church built hospitals and orphanages, and its *cofradías* (brotherhoods) were instrumental in the provision of welfare services to the poor and needy. Not only did these religious associations fulfill their basic duties of arranging town festivals in honor of saints and ensuring the observance of Christian morals, but they also behaved like charitable groups by providing free labor and money to their immediate communities in times of crisis.[30,31] In addition to these charitable and social imports, Catholic missionaries appended the Western notion of *kawanggawa* (charity) to the Filipino dictionary of doing good.[32]

The American colonial government further facilitated the progression of Philippine civil society in its resemblance to contemporary nonprofit organizations and foundations. Under the Americans, secularism flourished, demarcating boundaries between state and church, as well as between state and non-governmental provision of public goods and services.[33,34] As a result, the Philippines witnessed the emergence of secular welfare agencies, interest groups, professional associations, and charitable institutions. During this period youth, labor, peasant, and women's organizations flourished, alongside the creation of professional groups such as the Philippine Medical Association and the Philippine Bar Association.[35] More sophisticated, larger organizations with written constitutions—such as the Society of the Poor—also came into being.[36] Furthermore, Americans brought over to the Philippines their own non-government organizations like the American Red Cross and the Anti-Tuberculosis Society, which were known to receive philanthropic support from the local elite.[37,38] The Philippine Corporation Law of 1906 further encouraged nonprofit groups by giving them legal recognition along with proactive government funding (2.2 percent of the government's annual expenditure at the time) for local associations that focused on health services.[39]

In the 1960s and 1970s, the hopelessly deteriorating economy and increasingly rampant corruption of the Marcos regime triggered the mobilization of numerous social movements across sectors, from students to human rights advocacy.[40] Eventually, these movements gradually evolved into formal non-governmental organizations, supplementing the lack of government presence in delivering essential social services in certain areas of the country.[41,42] With these trends, civil society in the Philippines took its unified shape for the first time via protest and calls for reform against the authoritarian Marcos government. Marcos responded in 1972 with martial law, until public protests finally ousted him from power in 1986.

The subsequent Corazon Aquino administration enacted legislation favorable to nonprofits. The 1987 constitution explicitly stipulates the rights of non-governmental organizations, so that the state must respect their participation. With this new legal framework, registered NGOs rose by an astonishing 96 percent in less than a year, from 27,100 in early 1986 to 53,000 by late September.[43] And as José Magadia points out, civil society in the Philippines changed its focal orientation from resistant advocacy to a variety of other issues primarily in social services. With this shift in its fundamental identity, the overall sector was able to grow further by incorporating additional functions such as policy research, network building, and so forth.[44]

Income inequality, poverty, corruption, and ineffective public policy still plague the Philippines. In multiple socioeconomic indices and measurements, the country fares poorly, generally situating at the bottom half and lower tier. On the Social Progress Index, which attempts to capture how well countries provide basic social and environmental needs of their citizens, the Philippines ranks 68th out of 133 countries—even below its neighboring Southeast Asian nations of Malaysia and Thailand.[45] On the latest Corruption Perceptions Index, the Philippines ranks 95th out of

168 countries, scoring behind the likes of China, India, Indonesia, Malaysia, and Thailand.[46] Nevertheless, the fact that the Philippines hosts the largest number of NGOs per capita in Asia, between a quarter and half a million groups in total, reflects centuries of cultured yearning for doing good—and for civic engagement as a positive opportunity for the future.

South Korea

Many observers say that modern Korean civil society began 20 years ago, in the aftermath of twentieth-century industrialization and democratization. Industrialization came first (the "Han River Miracle," after World War II), then, in 1987, the June Democratic Uprising against military governments shaped the state and society that followed.[47]

But the practice of doing good, and its institutionalized forms in civil society, long predated these events in Korea. Many such practices began with Confucianism, which has contributed enormously to present-day Korean culture, perhaps more so than in any other Asian community.[48] As far back as the sixteenth century, Confucianism in Korea gave birth to private academies that taught ethics. These academies were essentially the equivalent of a modern-day NGO. They grew locally without any involvement and support from the state, instead funded through donations from local elites.[49] And they demonstrated a high level of management autonomy and independence from the state. For example, the academies faced no interference from the government, neither in regulating their student admission policies nor in their economic plans to rent their lands to tenant farmers for self-funding.[50] Unfortunately, tight oversight of these academies arrived under King Yeongjo in the eighteenth century, in the name of accomplishing "grand harmony," ultimately stalling the growth of this premature sector of society.[51]

Japanese colonialism had mixed effects on Korean civil society. Indirectly, it encouraged modern development, ending Korea's feudal society and introducing capitalism.[52] It was also during this period that Korea had its first private scholarship foundation, Yangyounghoe, established in 1939.[53] But Japan's aim to solidify control over the Korean peninsula involved cracking down on any form of social movements that challenged its colonial rule.[54,55] Due to the hostile relationship between the colonial ruler and the Korean people, Koreans began to regard the regime more as an illegitimate alien power than as a moral patriarch like their past imperial rulers.[56] This antagonistic anti-state orientation is constantly echoed throughout much of Korea's history during the twentieth century and defines the fundamental identity of Korean civil society to this day.

Independence from Japanese colonialism in 1945 enabled the brief growth of previously repressed social movements. Farmers, the poor, and other marginalized groups of society eventually congregated under an umbrella organization named *Chonnong* whose membership reached 3 million people in 1946.[57] Service-oriented religious groups and charity were also for the first time introduced to the country during this period.[58] This sudden expansion of civil society in Korea can be attributed to the lack of an official government for three weeks after liberation, which provided room for a high degree of freedom and autonomy that these movements had never experienced during the colonial era.[59,60] However, this brief period of optimism for the charitable sector was cut short by the arrival of the first authoritarian ruler in modern Korean history, followed by a series of subsequent military dictatorships.

Three extremely powerful rulers dominated the next 40 years of the post-liberation Republic of Korea: Rhee Syngman (1948–1960), Park Chung-hee (1963–1979), and Chun Doo-hwan (1980–1988). Korean civil society's anti-state disposition further intensified under their rule, chafing against the military support that kept the presidents in power.[61] This confrontational relationship meant advocacy groups, serving as the representative voice of the disgruntled citizenry, came to lead the nonprofit sector in Korea.[62,63]

Even so, other kinds of social service organizations managed to flourish amid the tensions. Under President Rhee Syngman, non-political service-oriented organizations backed by foreign aid were relatively free to pursue their welfare activities. After the coup that installed President Park Chung-hee, Korea saw a rise in the standard of living, as Park's regime was both authoritarian and development-oriented. The resulting growth of the middle class enabled the development of such organizations as the *Saemaul* (New Village) Movement. Now regarded as one of the most well-known legacies of the Park regime, the New Village Movement played a huge role in the urbanization and development of Korean local agricultural communities, implementing the central government's policies and plans at a grassroots level.[64] Completely rehabilitating rural infrastructure from top to bottom, the New Village Movement is now considered a "classic example of community-driven development."[65]

Park's development-driven agenda came to fruition under his successor Chun Doo-hwan, another military dictator, in the 1980s. That decade brought rapid industrialization, urbanization, and socioeconomic class diversification, which in turn led to popular support for various civil society organizations (from women's groups to environmental advocacy groups). Such organizations played active roles in anti-state efforts to bring down the military dictator, until Chun eventually stepped down in the face of ongoing public demonstrations and protests.[66]

Those 40 years of authoritarianism shaped the advocacy-focused, anti-state nature of Korean civil society. Even today, the most influential and prominent organizations are advocacy groups concerned with issues such as the environment, women's rights, and social justice.[67] Now there are 7600 such organizations, the majority of which were founded in the 1990s. And, in the words of Bidet, authoritarian governments' "instrumentalization" of non-governmental organizations and civil society groups whose activities and projects were well in line with their policy objectives also laid the foundation for various SDOs and the overall nonprofit sector.

That legacy also presents Korea with particular challenges. Donors recognize Korean civil society's heavy sway toward advocacy groups, and that makes some wary; many philanthropists (usually *chaebol*, the Korean term for family dominated conglomerates) are reluctant to donate their money to charity and partner with local NGOs, alternatively seeking to work by themselves via private foundations or to work together with the government.[68] This distrust is not one-sided. Because Korea's wealthy elite traditionally maintained close ties with military regimes, their lack of civic participation against authoritarianism makes them remnants of authoritarianism. The recent scandal of Korean conglomerates' shady donations to former President Park Geun-hye has reaffirmed this suspicion of Korean society against the wealthy, exacerbating distrust between the people and potential philanthropists.

China

China's development of charity and philanthropy is often misconstrued to be anemic. With its one-party political system and a widespread assumption that civil society is inherently a Western value and concept, this is understandable. Before the current Communist Party rule, the Chinese moved from one imperial regime to another, casting shadow over a rich culture of self-help. But China has a long history of doing good.

Confucianism introduced China to basic concepts of community care, from taking care of the elderly to providing education to the youth. This provision of welfare predated any formal institutionalization of social welfare and civil society, but it was to be taken up primarily by the government acting as the father figure of the people.[69] But the officials of the Qin dynasty disagreed. They advocated for a strong state and a weak society, neglecting the state's civic duty to attend to the poor, believing that those in need were at fault for their own poverty. Chinese citizenry stepped forward to fill this gap, creating the country's first systematic private form of charity: family-based kinship organizations. These family self-help groups were both a reaction to the legalist Qin regime that failed to provide social services and a reflection of existing Confucian principles that emphasized community care in terms of family relations.

These lineage organizations provided public goods and services, including care for widows and orphans, distribution of grain, and construction of schools.[70] Wealthy individuals—most notably, salt moguls—oversaw village social welfare activities.[71] These clan-based groups gradually spread from just southeast coastal China to the rest of the country during the Song (960–1279) and Qing (1644–1912) dynasties. The nature of these groups also changed at the same time, easing their blood-tied membership requirements and focusing more on the delivery of social services.[72] Family-based groups continued to flourish after the end of imperial dynasties, and other types of civic organizations arose, including professional associations and foundations.[73]

The smooth uptrend in China's growing civil society halted after the Communist Party came to power. The Communist Party cracked down on all private associations, seeing them as a sign of state failure.[74] The repression of these organizations, along with late exposure to key concepts pertaining to charity, shaped current misconceptions of Chinese civil society.

Despite this unfriendly environment for the third sector, another term for civil society, during the twentieth century, Deng Xiaoping's open-door economic policies enabled the beginning of contemporary charity and philanthropy. In 1995, an NGO Forum held alongside the Fourth World Conference on Women in Beijing introduced the general public and the government to the term "NGO" for the first time.[75] With this occasion, the Communist Party accepted that NGOs were not anti-governmental opposition groups.

NGOs and civil society ended up aligning well with Deng's free-market ideology. The growing popularity of a liberalized Chinese economy crept into the field of social services, applying free-market principles to social welfare and allowing room for the third sector to take up a much more influential role in delivering public goods and services to the people. Hence, during the second half of the 1990s, China experienced a huge surge in the number of large domestic charity organizations, such as Friends of Nature and Global Villages, as well as the entry of many foreign NGOs.[76]

Under the Hu Jintao government, charities faced a brief period of restrictions, as Beijing became wary of NGOs bringing forth ideologies challenging to the Communist Party.[77] At this time, government-organized programs, such as the China Red Cross, rose to prominence and became dominant forces within the sector.[78] The Chinese government also reverted to more involvement in the provision of social goods and services, ending various market initiatives begun in the 1990s.

Amidst this recent experience of government pushback, other challenges to the growth of Chinese philanthropy arose in the form of nationwide scandals and controversial legislations.

Most notable was the 2011 Guo Meimei scandal, in which a young Chinese woman who claimed to be the "commercial general manager" of the "China Red Cross Chamber of Commerce" flaunted her lavish lifestyle of luxury sports cars and branded bags on social media. It caused such public uproar that domestic charitable organizations saw a 90-percent drop in donations.[79,80] This particular scandal exacerbated the lack of institutionalized trust in China, which heavily relies on *guanxi* (strong personal connections).[81] The World Values Survey, for example, indicates that close to 80 percent of the Chinese respondents do not trust strangers.[82] The Guo Meimei scandal further reduced the low level of institutionalized trust resulting from the culture of *guanxi* and societal distrust. Such scandals and their ramifications remain one of the biggest obstacles to the success of Chinese civil society.

The 2016 Charity Law put forth by the National People's Congress may shape the next set of relationships between the government and nonprofit organizations. Its impact is not yet clear. Supporters see improvements made in registration, fundraising, and tax incentives, while critics worry about restrictions on overseas NGOs.[83,84,85,86] The Charity Law, its implications, and potential effects will be discussed in greater detail in a later chapter of this book.

China's long experience with charity and philanthropy brings context to the challenge given at the start of this section: yes, the United States boasts philanthropic giving 21 times larger than in China, with a GDP only twice as large, but that does not mean China is not interested in giving.[87] China has a rich history of the wealthy giving back to society in the form of clan-based lineage organizations. Civil society proved resilient to a temporary downturn during the twentieth-century Communist rule and now is developing at a good pace. The following facts suggest an optimistic future:[88,89,90]

1. China has experienced a 66-percent increase in the total amount of charitable donations during the time span of 2009–2014.
2. Five times as many charitable organizations were in China by 2014, compared with ten years earlier.
3. Per capita charitable giving increased by 20 percent annually through 2013.
4. 2014 saw $15.51 billion worth of total regular donations, even excluding one-off donations made for natural disasters.

Taiwan

Modern Taiwan, founded after the Chinese Communist Party took full control of the Mainland in 1949, began as the Chinese Nationalist Party—or the Kuomintang (KMT)—fled to the island of Formosa. Prior to this KMT exodus, and before 50 years of Japanese colonialism, Taiwan was part of the Qing dynasty from 1683 to 1895.[91] Under Qing influence, Taiwan gradually accustomed itself to Chinese cultural traditions, including Confucianism. Taiwan's culture of doing good long resembled that of Mainland China, while its recent state-civil society relations resembled that in South Korea due to the shared experience of having an authoritarian, developmental regime.

Yet Taiwan's culture is unique. It differs from its Mainland counterpart in the more significant role that Buddhism plays in charity and philanthropy. The Buddhist notions of *karma* and accumulating merit in particular galvanize the Taiwanese people to volunteer and donate. In multiple surveys, more than 50 percent of the respondents have directly attributed their motivation behind doing good to avoiding bad *karma* and accumulating merit.[92,93] In fact, one of the most well-known and largest charitable institutions in Taiwan is a global Buddhist organization known as the Buddhist Compassion Relief Tzu Chi Foundation, the largest owner of private land in the country.[94,95] This mix of Taiwan's Confucian roots and the widespread Buddhist faith and practices encouraging benevolent activities attests to Taiwan's societal capacity for doing good. Many believe that the Tzu Chi Foundation, whose assets are not publicly disclosed, is the wealthiest foundation in Asia.

Taiwan has also been shaped by military dictatorship for more than 30 years after 1947. This period, marked by rapid economic growth and industrialization, has been dubbed the "Taiwan Miracle." In the first half of this time, the KMT government solidified its control over the island, supervising and controlling the public arena with military might. Any demands or suggestions coming from society were met with suppression and censorship. Martial law put Taiwan under authoritarian rule for the next 38 years. Civil society became hard to imagine.

From 1963 to 1978, economic policies started to top the list of priorities for the KMT.[96] Shifting the economy to one based on export-oriented industrialization, the KMT inadvertently gave birth to and bolstered the urban middle and industrial working classes. For the first time, public life saw the influence of other societal interests—market forces—besides the military political party. However, the KMT still exercised its dominance, and many of the economic players displayed political loyalty to the KMT for business opportunities.[97] Competing views of society were limited to a few intellectuals and social elites.[98] Civil society remained in limbo.

In the 1980s, numerous social movements began to emerge, not as a unified opposition to the KMT but rather as a reflection of diverse interests and socioeconomic classes resulting from economic growth.[99] Without this united front, and given the KMT's self-organized transition from "hard" authoritarianism to "soft" authoritarianism, co-opting the voices of Taiwanese civil society, Taiwan avoided the kind of direct confrontation seen in Korea's June Democratic Uprising of 1987.[100,101] While Korea's military regime violently cracked down on dissident groups, the KMT in Taiwan eased toward democratization.[102] With the co-opting of the third sector, social movements and civil society groups did not feel the necessity of confronting the government, but were instead inclined to engage with the state through formal mechanisms and channels set forth by the government.

This is not to say that there were no protests and public demonstrations against the government. In 1987, up to 1800 street demonstrations were recorded.[103] As with Korea, authoritarianism amid a growing prosperity shaped civil society in Taiwan, so it began to be, and remains, advocacy-oriented. On the other hand, the KMT's self-democratization led to a more constructive relationship between the state and the third sector, mutually reinforcing the democratization process and providing a much more favorable environment for the growth of the charitable sector in the country.

This state-civil society cooperation reached its all-time high after the lifting of martial law in 1987. The Taiwanese government started to embrace and collaborate with these social movements, allowing formal establishment of NGOs.[104] The third sector and the private sector began to be included as consultants in the legislation of policies, laws, and regulations. Furthermore, the nonprofit sector in Taiwan has taken an even more active role in its state-society relationship by engaging in foreign policy. In the context of Taiwan's unique cross-strait relations with China, Taiwan's Ministry of Foreign Affairs and civil society have cooperated with participation in international conferences.[105] Nonprofit organizations are in effect acting to promote Taiwan's soft power abroad. With this friendly infrastructure and environment acquired after overcoming many historical obstacles, Taiwan now boasts nearly 60,000[106] registered non-governmental organizations as of 2015, reflecting the growth and vibrancy of the sector.

Japan

Japan's civil society is an anomaly in the Asian continent. Japan as a nation is not well known for charity and philanthropy, despite its status as the most developed economy in the region. Frequently cited reasons range from the Japanese population's cultural disposition of deference to the state, and corporations to the developmental regime's tight regulatory and political oversight.[107,108] These analyses of Japan's underdeveloped sector of doing good touch on material truths. What is missing in this discourse, however, is an acknowledgment of Japan's proven record, from ancient times to today, of helping others in the community.

Japanese philanthropy dates back to at least the seventh and eighth centuries, when members of the affluent noble class and high-ranking monks established charitable projects and institutions under major Buddhist temples such as the Tōdai-ji and Shitennō-ji.[109] Buddhist temples initiated fundraising campaigns, known as *Kanjin*, to finance religious activities and social welfare initiatives.[110] Catholicism, which arrived in Japan during the sixteenth century, further exposed the country to the concept of doing good. Catholic missionaries founded mutual aid organizations called *Misericordia* to raise funds for social service projects such as building nursing homes and leprosy hospitals.[111,112]

Homegrown Japanese philanthropy developed further in the Edo period (1603–1868). First, wealthy Osaka-based merchants established private academies backed by an endowment system, laying the grounds for

Japan's modern-day foundations, *zaidan hojin*.[113] Most notably, in 1829, a purveyor to the feudal lord of Akita offered *Kan-on-kō*—land purchased for agricultural production whose proceeds went to assist local peasants and orphans. This philanthropic gesture, later joined by an additional 191 donors, exists to this day as a social welfare organization.

These cases of religious and institutionalized giving remained relatively isolated, however. Central authorities' long history of monopolizing the provision of public goods and social services left little room for civil society to grow beyond its beginning stage.[114] The highly centralized public sector continued through the Meiji Restoration in the late nineteenth century. The Civil Code was established in 1898, legally recognizing and systematizing for the first time the existence of private nonprofit activities (the *koeki hojin* system).[115] But the Meiji government's successful import of Western technology and culture into Japanese society provided the foundation of a modernized state. Japan then rose as a major imperial power in Asia, flexing economic and military dominance throughout the region from the 1920s to the 1940s. During this period of military authoritarianism, all private entities were merged into one single national organization under government pressure and supervision.[116]

After Japan's defeat in World War II, the war-torn island, faced with the challenge to quickly recover the economy, employed heavy central planning executed by its elite bureaucracy. This interventionist developmental state and its influential bureaucracy are key to explaining the current perception of Japanese civil society.

The developmental state imposed legal restrictions and encroaching managerial oversight on the nonprofit sector. The Civil Code covering each *koeki hojin* (public interest corporation) requires that an applying organization have its license granted by a government agency, contradicting the "non-governmental" part of NGOs.[117] The application process is difficult and complex, with many facets advancing the government's agenda. For example, NGOs were made accountable to the practice of *amakudari* (translated literally as "descent from heaven"), pressuring NGOs to hire retired bureaucrats.[118] Persistent requests for detailed accounts and activity reports and internal meddling of NGOs' day-to-day operations became common.[119]

What allowed the bureaucracy's dominance over civil society to continue? The government delivered on its promises pertaining to economic development, and in response, the Japanese citizenry regarded the progress made by the developmental state in a positive light. In other words, public trust in the bureaucracy further empowered its role in managing the Japanese economy and society, leaving the state's overbearing governance of the nonprofit sector to continue without challenge.[120] Added to this "performance legitimacy" was Japan's long history of deference to the state.[121] Japanese even has a self-deprecating phrase expressing a sense of reverence for the bureaucracy, ***kansonminpi*** (translated literally as "respectful bureaucracy, despiteful common people").[122] Keiko Hirata cites Confucianism's emphasis on social stability, preference of the larger group over individuals, and hierarchical organization of society as the cultural motive behind the Japanese people's deference to the state. This wariness of dissident opinions against the government reached its peak during the Cold War era, when many anti-government NGOs and individuals were alleged to be communist or radically left-wing. With Japan's winning streak of economic growth, and the preexisting Japanese tendency to follow the bureaucracy, the state's constant intervention in the nonprofit sector remained intact for most of the twentieth century.

Recent socioeconomic circumstances have changed the nature of state-civil society relations in Japan, hinting at the possibility of an unforeseen growth trajectory for the nonprofit sector. The fruits of the developmental state—more middle-class citizens, more wealth, and more educational opportunities—have stimulated the expansion of civil society in Japan.[123] Likewise, globalization has also contributed to the inception of Japan's young civil society. The developmental state naturally felt pressure to meet in line with the standards of the developed world and international norms favoring the concept of civil society.[124]

The government's changing attitude toward the charitable sector grew after two major earthquakes in 1995 (Kobe) and 2011 (Tohoku). The Kobe earthquake—with 6500 dead and 75,000 buildings demolished—was especially damaging, and the response telling.[125] Despite heroic stories of volunteerism, the overall coordination among the state, civil society, and thousands of volunteers was disorganized, failing to respond to the disaster in an efficient manner.[126] Stringent registration laws for nonprofit organizations prevented the government from seamlessly communicating with small-scale organizations that convened in Kobe.[127] At the same time, petty internal power struggles within the bureaucracy aggravated the situation at hand.[128] This administrative disaster, betraying the people's trust in the bureaucracy, served as an impetus for a series of regulatory and policy changes conducive to the growth of civil society. The 1998 NPO (nonprofit organization) Law eased requirements for registration, and in

2002 the government began engaging academics and NGOs on discussing plans to reform the entire legal framework for civil society.[129]

Coupled with this renewed attitude of the government toward the nonprofit sector in the aftermath of the Kobe earthquake were changing social circumstances. Most significantly, the issue of Japan's aging society amidst a limited welfare state is creating new opportunities for NGOs, regarded by the government as a cost-effective alternative to provide essential social services to the elderly.[130]

In terms of individual giving, institutionalized philanthropy, and the nonprofit sector, Japan lags behind its regional counterparts in Asia. However, like many other Asian nations, Japan has committed acts of great charity over many centuries. Today, Japan shows that it, too, can be benevolent, and now has a political and social infrastructure evolving to facilitate the growth of the sector.

Singapore

Singapore tops the charts in many socioeconomic measurements. Singaporeans boast a GDP per capita of $52,888.70, among the highest in the world.[131] They also enjoy a high quality of living, with a life expectancy of 83 and adult literacy rate of 96.8 percent.[132,133] Quality health care, education, and other social welfare benefits and programs are taken care of by the government. Where, in such a well-managed and tightly controlled landscape, is there room for philanthropic input? Much of the donated money goes abroad, and the aggregate number of donations is relatively low.[134,135] In fact, one of the few major players in philanthropic giving in Singapore is the Tote Board, a government-backed organization.[136] What input does come from the nonprofit sector is still heavily influenced by the state. The government's stance is generally adverse to NGOs, especially politically vocal ones.[137] As the primary caretaker of social services, Singapore's government fundamentally defines the role of doing good in its modern nation-state.

It was not always so. From 1819 to 1963, Singapore was under British colonial rule, with occupation by the Japanese empire from 1942 to 1945.[138] During this pre-independence era, civil society in Singapore was quite vibrant in the form of ethnic self-help organizations.[139] As authoritarian as it may have been, the British colonial government did not impede the indigenous growth of these groups and may have in fact indirectly created the room for civil society's growth through subpar provision of social services.[140,141] In the 1950s and 1960s, these groups contributed to Singapore's fight for independence.[142] Other types of associations, such as trade unions, student groups, and the women's movement started to flourish during this period as well.[143] Without the presence of an authoritarian government overtly adversarial to civil society and monopolizing the provision of welfare, pre-independence Singapore was able to experience a hint of nascent civil society.

After independence, the People's Action Party (PAP) led by Lee Kuan Yew reversed what could have been a continued sense of excitement around civil society. Two underlying beliefs framed the government's early contentious attitude toward civil society. First, the PAP believed that the public sphere in Singapore had been excessively politicized during the final few years of the colonial era, with groups and riots on ethnic and ideological lines interrupting social stability.[144] Second, the utmost priority of the government's policy agenda back then was economic development.[145] Successful accomplishment on this front was reflected in the government's efficient provision of public benefits, leaving no space and few opportunities for civil society groups.[146] From the perspective of the PAP, a powerful centralized government, superseding other segments of society, was absolutely crucial to maintaining both the social and the economic well-being of the newborn city-state.

The PAP imposed legal and "extra-legal" limits on civil society.[147] The Internal Security Act and the Societies Act were used to oppress any form of dissident voices and increase oversight of non-governmental entities.[148,149] More significant were the PAP government's political strategies and institutional barriers used to control and co-opt civil society. The party sought to delineate the public debate surrounding civil society by alternatively naming it as "civic" society, focusing more on the "responsibilities" of the citizenry rather than its "rights."[150] Having begun as a one-party state that unilaterally provided social services, the PAP shrewdly evolved into a "competitive authoritarian"[151] regime that still adhered to the principal belief of the government as the core of society, while allowing limited, state-controlled civil outreach.

When Goh Chok Tong became the country's second prime minister in 1990, he instilled a sense of hope among Singaporeans that Singapore may soon become a liberalized society.[152] At that time, Brigadier-General George Yeo, minister for information and the arts, gave a speech incorporating a metaphor apt for the current circumstances surrounding civil society in Singapore. He acknowledged past government policies and attitudes as resembling a "banyan tree" that gave no room for civil society to grow, calling for a "pruning" of the tree (yet keeping the tree as the core of society).[153]

But after losing four seats to the opposition in the 1991 general election, the PAP realized a more liberalized stance toward civil society did not result in more votes. Going forward, PAP gave less emphasis to its renewed state-civil society relations.[154] Nonetheless, the small step forward taken by the government tilted the vertical relationship toward an increased presence of civil society in Singapore. Voluntary welfare associations and SDOs were welcomed in a supplementary role; this was known as the "many helping hands" policy.[155] Although the Singaporean government might not be open to the idea of civil society opposed to the state, it is willing to accept a civil society supplementing the "pruned banyan tree" state.

The "pruned banyan tree" vision of state-civil society relations in Singapore applies to present-day affairs in the country. Philanthropic giving and charity organizations are welcomed, if not encouraged. Through the National Volunteer & Philanthropy Centre, for example, various nationwide giving events are hosted to encourage individual giving, and tax schemes are renewed to incentivize larger scale philanthropic gestures from the private sector.[156,157] With this continued acceptance by the government of the philanthropic and charitable community, the city-state's private sector and culture of giving and helping others might be on a more positive track for the future.

Hong Kong

Hong Kong, like Singapore, is an Asian city-state whose history is primarily characterized by British colonialism and rapid economic development. But the story of Hong Kong's philanthropy and charity differs due to its proximity and unique historical ties to China. Hong Kong also has a less interventionist government, allowing its social delivery sector to take a much more prominent role than its Singaporean counterpart. The history of doing good in Hong Kong has been shaped by these three primary factors: British colonialism, Chinese influence, and a laissez-faire state.

In colonizing Hong Kong, the British Empire sought to provide its merchants with a physical port of access to China but not necessarily to spread Christianity nor to "civilize" the local population, as it had done in its other colonies.[158] With this narrower goal in mind, the British colonial government limited its involvement in the day-to-day affairs of Hong

Kong society.[159] Such "positive non-interventionism" profoundly impacted the nonprofit community.[160]

The British government neglected to provide education and health care, leaving room for Hong Kong's first nonprofit groups to emerge.[161] These organizations divided into two types, Christian-inspired missionary charities and Chinese clan-based associations.[162,163] In pursuit of converting the local citizens to Christianity, missionaries ended up providing schools, hospitals, orphanages, and even elderly care facilities. Chinese clan-based associations, known as *kaifong*, mobilized neighborhoods for mutual aid to fill the void left by the "small" British colonial government. They built the Man Mo Temple, launched by a few wealthy members of the Chinese community, and the Tung Wah Hospital.[164]

Even under British rule, Hong Kong remained in China's sphere of influence. Major events experienced by the Mainland—whether for good or for bad—had ramifications for Hong Kong. The aforementioned *kaifong* clan-based associations are one example of China's influence, and the number of these groups proliferated as Chinese refugees poured into the city in the wake of China's civil war between the Communist Party and the Nationalist Party.[165] The colonial government could not single-handedly tackle all of the social challenges and demands rising from this influx, increasing the need for NGOs' supplementary assistance. This period also saw the rise of *tung heung wui* ("same-village associations," in English), formed by people who wanted to help those hailing from the same place of origin in China.[166] It is still quite common for donors from Hong Kong to provide charitable support for projects in their home villages despite having left those places generations ago.[167]

It was also during this time that several NGOs and philanthropic organizations now well known in Hong Kong society were established. The Hong Kong Council of Social Service, a network of NGOs, was founded in 1947 to help coordinate the activities of these proliferating self-help organizations, and the Hong Kong Jockey Club declared its commitment to donate its annual surpluses for philanthropy.[168] Both organizations are key intermediaries in the industry of doing good in Hong Kong today.

Especially since the 1997 "handover," China's influence continues to shape Hong Kong's civil society. In recent years, the unique political relationship of "one country, two systems" has prompted the formation of more advocacy groups, both in opposition to and in support of the Chinese government.[169,170]

Both the British and the Chinese influence developed against a backdrop of a laissez-faire government. Modern-day Hong Kong is a special administrative region, a city-state commonly known for a vibrant private sector, low tax schemes, and detached government involvement in social services. The government's regulatory framework for NGOs is neutral, not interfering with the formal establishment of such organizations and at the same time, not incentivizing further beyond the provisions of the Inland Revenue Ordinance pertaining to tax exemption.[171] Private options for any social needs are readily made available to the Hong Kong population.

Officially, Hong Kong relies on free-market principles when it comes to delivering public welfare, and it certainly does so in comparison to Singapore. That is, the government is clearly not the main provider of social services. Nevertheless, the Hong Kong government now is the single largest source of funding for NGOs, providing 28 percent of their operating budgets.[172] This funding occurs in response to pressure to spend more on public welfare, in the wake of rapid economic development and persistent income inequality.[173,174] Given its dedication to a non-interventionist free market, yet attending to the demands of its people, the Hong Kong government has contracted out to SDOs the primary role of providing social services. Hong Kong's state-civil society relationship is one of supplementary mutual dependence, where a rise in the state's indirect spending on social welfare increases the size of the voluntary sector as well.[175] Budget cuts have the opposite effect, and with recent financial crises, the Hong Kong government has decreased its funding for SDOs.[176] Competition for government funding within the sector has thus intensified, and fundraising has been identified by numerous organizations to be the most difficult current challenge.[177]

Thailand

Three historical experiences have defined the modern-day landscape of Thailand's charity and philanthropy. First, religious giving—particularly in the context of Buddhism—has been and still is a major part of the nationwide philanthropic culture. Second, Thailand's unique position as the only country in Southeast Asia not colonized by either Europe or Japan has implications for its social sector. Third, Thailand's current domestic challenges, including multiple military coups and regime changes, have contributed to an extreme politicization of its civil society. The cumulative result of these historical events is a relatively recent emergence of the nonprofit sector and a leaning within the sector toward advocacy-oriented social movements. Only recently have socioeconomic trends, including income equality, begun to encourage development of SDOs and social enterprises.

For centuries, Buddhism has functioned as the philanthropic epicenter of Thailand.[178] Individual giving to both the religious order, Sangha, and to those in need helped acquire merit and to meet the moral standards expected of a Buddhist.[179] Thais have long placed water jars outside their homes for thirsty individuals, and strangers commonly found free housing and food from welcoming village residents.[180] Buddhist temples used donations for providing education, elderly care, and health care to their local communities, and they still play a pivotal role for doing good in Thailand.[181]

Thailand's civil society has also been shaped by its independence, as the sole Asian kingdom never colonized by foreign empires in the nineteenth and early twentieth centuries.[182] Britain and France agreed to leave the nation as a buffer between their Asian spheres of influence. Two monarchs during this period maneuvered to preserve the balance, engaging with as many foreign delegations as possible via trade treaties. The two kings also opened the country to foreign influences by sending Thai aristocrats abroad to European institutions. By 1940, Thailand boasted a well-developed infrastructure, including roads, canals, railways, shipyards, hospitals, and schools.[183] This might have partially contributed to the relatively late inception of the nonprofit sector in Thailand during the later years of the twentieth century, which offered an opening for organized civil society organizations only after the democratic transition.[184]

A more telling legacy is that of a powerful bureaucratic and military elite in Bangkok. Discouraged by the deteriorating royal class, this new elite staged a coup in 1932, paving the grounds for Thailand's cycle of future military coups.[185] Under control-conscious military rule, there was little room for Thailand's civil society to grow. During and after World War II, the government used the National Culture Act of 1942 and similar laws to control Chinese clan-based philanthropic associations, in the name of fighting communism from China.[186] For much of the twentieth century, the authoritarian military state continued to view with suspicion any organized form of private interests.

Thailand's first major civilian resistance against military dominance occurred in 1973, when 500,000 students came to the streets of Bangkok to protest for democracy, eventually forcing the government leaders to leave the country.[187] Though military rule returned afterwards, the student protests and the increasing number of NGOs forced the military to believe that it had to work together with civil society for its own survival.[188] As a result, Thailand saw an increase in the expression of social demands and in the number of grassroots organizations during the 1980s.[189] However, under the unstable seesawing back and forth between military regimes and civilian rule, civil society in Thailand became ever more politicized and advocacy-oriented.[190,191,192]

Indonesia

Through its sheer size, abundance of natural resources, and rapidly growing population, Indonesia is elevating its macroeconomic status to a point where it is now a part of the four emerging "MINT"[193] economies, alongside Mexico, Nigeria, and Turkey. Beneath this economic growth, however, are alarming indicators of poverty: more than half of the population still lives on less than two dollars a day, 29 out of every 1000 children die before the age of five, and the maternal death rate remains stubbornly high.[194] Indonesia has long had such disparities of wealth, and its social sector has sought to fill the gap. Charity and philanthropy in Indonesia has encountered much support in the process, along with various roadblocks, in keeping with the country's unique cultural background.

Religion, particularly Islam and its cultural customs, occupies a prominent place in the Indonesian context of doing good. With more than 85 percent of the country professing Islamic faith,[195,196] *zakat* (almsgiving), alongside non-obligatory forms of charity, defines the nature of individual philanthropy in Indonesia. Almost all Muslim Indonesians fulfill their *zakat* duties annually, and more than 90 percent of individual giving in Indonesia is accounted by religious giving.[197,198] Amid this prevalence of Islamic philanthropy, institutionalized collection and administration of *zakat* funds came to the fore, both from the public sector and from the private sector. In 1949, the Ministry of Religious Affairs was founded; it later adopted the role of managing *zakat* funds, and private collecting agencies known as Lazis (*Lembaga Amil Zakat*) followed suit.[199,200,201]

Christianity also plays a role. Though less than ten percent of the population practices Christianity, the religion's commitment to delivering social services (including emergency disaster relief, education, and health care) make it a notable contributor. So does its follower base of wealthy and/or ethnic Chinese Indonesians.[202,203]

The religious backdrop does not always promote a positive environment for social services. Under the authoritarian Suharto government, many religious impulses were steered toward containing communism and cracking down on dissident political voices.[204,205] Also, giving donations to non-religious NGOs—even those for social services—is less commonplace, and donating to non-Islamic organizations is even shunned.[206]

Religious and nonreligious NGOs developed under Dutch colonial rule.[207] The Dutch government intervened little in private matters related to *zakat*, unintentionally allowing for the emergence of Islamic associations.[208,209,210,211] To the dismay of the Dutch empire, Indonesian civil society grew toward social consciousness and a sector-wide goal of fighting for independence.[212,213,214] With its clear division of public and private spheres, the Dutch colonial government enabled a freer Islamic philanthropic life that led to the establishment of community organizations.

The charitable sector faced a less tolerant government in the New Order era (1965–1998) under General Suharto. Suharto suppressed any dissent, halting the growth of NGOs and other civil society organizations in the country.[215,216] He co-opted religious activities for his agenda, as noted above, and limited other functions.[217,218] Hans Antlöv, Rustam Ibrahim, and Peter van Tuijl aptly summarize the position of civil society in the New Order era:

> During more than three decades of authoritarian rule, civil society in Indonesia was seen as a part of the problem, not as the solution. Civil society was there to be controlled, not to be listened to or as a partner to work with.[219]

At best, alongside religious groups, only community development-focused NGOs—locally known as *Lembaga Swadaya Masyarakat*, meaning "self-reliant community development institution"—were recognized by the government as in line with its development activities and policies.[220] The legacy of this predatory food chain between the public sector and the social sector resonates across the country to this day, where some Suharto-era laws are still applicable and readily made available should the government deem necessary in its intent to control civil society.[221]

In the final years of the Suharto regime, and following its fall in 1998, political democratization resulted in an increase in the number of NGOs from thousands to tens of thousands just by the end of 2003.[222,223,224] However, a wide array of current challenges and obstacles remains for the charitable and philanthropic sector in Indonesia. Indonesia lacks any major incentive for this sector, in that tax exemptions for NGOs are not provided; nor are tax deductions for individual donors.[225,226] Charitable organizations rely heavily on foreign funding, given a lack of vibrant domestic philanthropy.[227] And in the wake of the politicized struggles under the Suharto regime, distrust remains high between the private, public, and nonprofit sectors.[228,229] These areas can be improved with efforts by all relevant stakeholders in Indonesian society, tackling its challenges with the combined efforts of NGOs, the government, and the private sector.

Malaysia

The Malaysian experience of philanthropy is history in the making. That is, with its semi-authoritarian regime and stiffly divided multiethnic populace, Malaysia did not see a vibrant third sector until recently.[230, 231] Several factors inhibited the birth and growth of active charity, while recent changes bring a hint of hope for a slowly developing field.

Malaysia's "semi-authoritarian" label reflects the mismatch between its official status as a democratic nation and its reality as a one-party state.[232,233] Based on repressive legislative measures, some would argue that Malaysia is simply authoritarian.[234] Civil society has been particularly restrained by the 1960 Internal Security Act and the 1966 Societies Act, which permit detaining without trial and categorizes NGOs as "friendly" or "political."[235,236] The government has also established its own social organizations, including the National Human Rights Commission and the Federation of Malaysian Consumer Organizations, to absorb the functions of social movements and NGOs.[237]

In sharp contrast to the Dutch Indonesian experience of separate private and public spheres of Islam, Malaysia's authoritarian reach influenced religious philanthropic life. The difference stems from a British colonial legacy, one that elevated the status of sultans at the expense of religious institutions.[238] Such a co-optation of religious affairs continued to exist throughout the post-colonial period; even the administration and collection of *zakat* is singlehandedly managed by governmental religious councils.[239] In such an unfavorable environment, it is surprising that some NGOs and civic activities exist at all.

An authoritarian state also complicated relationships among Malaysia's multiethnic populace. Federal discrimination and ensuing ethnic tensions encouraged segregation of philanthropic beneficiary groups and a fractured civil society.[240,241] In particular, Elizabeth Cogswell finds in her survey of civil society that in Malaysia, Chinese help Chinese, Malays help Malays, and Indians help Indians. While charitable organizations might state in their charters that they serve without regard to ethnicity, in practice some focused on assisting their ethnic groups in response to the government's discriminatory policies.[242] Sometimes, a given ethnic group would even refuse help from another due to historical tensions.[243] Chinese Malaysians, seeing the preferential treatment of Malays, often donated in China to their villages and communities of origin, rather than to other fellow Malaysians in need of assistance.[244]

Despite these challenges, recent affairs in Malaysia attest to potential. With increased exposure to uncensored social media and the Internet, Malaysians are demanding more in terms of political liberalization.[245] Such desire burst forth when the dominant United Malays National Organization party suffered a heavy defeat in the 2008 elections, leading for the first time to a united electoral front within civil society against the government regardless of ethnicity.[246] The transition might not come easily, given the lack of political experience among now-elected social leaders.[247] Nonetheless, if these new members of the government promote productive reforms, charity and philanthropy in Malaysia may grow faster than ever before.

Notes

1. Peng, Jianmei. *China Charitable Giving Report.* China Charity Information Center, Beijing, China, 2014, p. 25.
2. "India's Poverty Profile." The World Bank, 27 May 2016. Web. 19 Apr. 2017. http://www.worldbank.org/en/news/infographic/2016/05/27/india-s-poverty-profile
3. Iyengar, Rishi. "India's Cash Crisis Left It with 11 Fewer Billionaires." *CNN Money.* Cable News Network, 7 Mar. 2017. Web. 20 Apr. 2017. http://money.cnn.com/2017/03/07/news/economy/india-billionaires-hurun-rich-list-demonetisation/
4. Sundar, Pushpa. "Philanthropy in the Building of Modern India." *Revealing Indian Philanthropy.* Eds. Mathieu Cantegreil, Dweep Chanana, and Ruth Kattumuri. London, United Kingdom: Alliance Publishing Trust, 2013, 31–43. Web. 20 Apr. 2017. https://www.ubs.com/content/dam/ubs/global/wealth_management/philanthropy_valuesbased_investments/indian-philanthrophy.pdf
5. Cantegreil, Mathieu, Dweep Chanana, and Ruth Kattumuri. "Understanding Giving in India." *Revealing Indian Philanthropy.* Eds. Mathieu Cantegreil,

Dweep Chanana, and Ruth Kattumuri. London, United Kingdom: Alliance Publishing Trust, 2013, 20–30. Web. 20 Apr. 2017. https://www.ubs.com/content/dam/ubs/global/wealth_management/philanthropy_valuesbased_investments/indian-philanthrophy.pdf

6. Maple, Terrie, and Richard Harrison. *India Giving: Insights into the Nature of Giving across India*. Rep. New Delhi, India: Charities Aid Foundation India, 2012. Web. 20 Apr. 2017. http://cafindia.org/images/CAF_India_launches_India_Giving_Report_2012.pdf. Recited from Cantegreil, Mathieu, Dweep Chanana, and Ruth Kattumuri. "Understanding Giving in India." *Revealing Indian Philanthropy*. Eds. Mathieu Cantegreil, Dweep Chanana, and Ruth Kattumuri. London, United Kingdom: Alliance Publishing Trust, 2013, 20–30. Web. 20 Apr. 2017. https://www.ubs.com/content/dam/ubs/global/wealth_management/philanthropy_valuesbased_investments/indian-philanthrophy.pdf
7. Viswanath, Priya, and Noshir Dadrawala. "Philanthropy and Equity: The Case of India." (2004): 1–31. Harvard Global Equity Initiative, 1 June 2004. Web. 20 Apr. 2017. https://www.cbd.int/financial/charity/india-phequity.pdf
8. Anderson, Leona. "Contextualizing Philanthropy in South Asia: A Textual Analysis of Sanskrit Sources." *Philanthropy in the World's Traditions*. Eds. Edward L. Queen II, Warren F. Ilchman, and Stanley N. Katz. N.p.: Indiana UP, 1998, 57–78. Print.
9. Sundar, Pushpa. "Philanthropy in the Building of Modern India." *Revealing Indian Philanthropy*. Eds. Mathieu Cantegreil, Dweep Chanana, and Ruth Kattumuri. London, United Kingdom: Alliance Publishing Trust, 2013, 31–43. Web. 20 Apr. 2017. https://www.ubs.com/content/dam/ubs/global/wealth_management/philanthropy_valuesbased_investments/indian-philanthrophy.pdf
10. "India | Discussion | History." *India Philanthropy Discussion | Coutts Million Dollar Donor Report*. Coutts, n.d. Web. 20 Apr. 2017. http://philanthropy.coutts.com/en/reports/2015/india/discussion.html
11. "Overview of Civil Society Organizations: India." (n.d.): n. pag. *Civil Society Briefs*. Asian Development Bank, June 2009. Web. 20 Apr. 2017. https://www.adb.org/sites/default/files/publication/28966/csb-ind.pdf
12. Sundar, Pushpa. "Philanthropy in the Building of Modern India." *Revealing Indian Philanthropy*. Ed. Mathieu Cantegreil, Dweep Chanana, and Ruth Kattumuri. London, United Kingdom: Alliance Publishing Trust, 2013, 31–43. Web. 20 Apr. 2017. https://www.ubs.com/content/dam/ubs/global/wealth_management/philanthropy_valuesbased_investments/indian-philanthrophy.pdf

13. "Overview of Civil Society Organizations: India." (n.d.): n. pag. *Civil Society Briefs*. Asian Development Bank, June 2009. Web. 20 Apr. 2017. https://www.adb.org/sites/default/files/publication/28966/csb-ind.pdf
14. Viswanath, Priya, and Noshir Dadrawala. "Philanthropy and Equity: The Case of India." (2004): 1–31. Harvard Global Equity Initiative, 1 June 2004. Web. 20 Apr. 2017. https://www.cbd.int/financial/charity/india-phequity.pdf
15. Sundar, Pushpa. "Philanthropy in the Building of Modern India." *Revealing Indian Philanthropy*. Eds. Mathieu Cantegreil, Dweep Chanana, and Ruth Kattumuri. London, United Kingdom: Alliance Publishing Trust, 2013, 31–43. Web. 20 Apr. 2017. https://www.ubs.com/content/dam/ubs/global/wealth_management/philanthropy_valuesbased_investments/indian-philanthrophy.pdf
16. Juergensmeyer, Mark, and Darrin M. McMahon. *Philanthropy in the World's Traditions*. Ed. Edward L. Queen II, Warren F. Ilchman, and Stanley N. Katz. N.p.: Indiana UP, 1998, 263–78. Print.
17. Quoted in R B Upadhyaya (1976) *Social Responsibility of Business and the Trusteeship Theory of Mahatma Gandhi* (Sterling Publishers, New Delhi) p vi. **Recited from** Sundar, Pushpa. "Philanthropy in the Building of Modern India." *Revealing Indian Philanthropy*. Eds. Mathieu Cantegreil, Dweep Chanana, and Ruth Kattumuri. London, United Kingdom: Alliance Publishing Trust, 2013, 31–43. Web. 20 Apr. 2017. https://www.ubs.com/content/dam/ubs/global/wealth_management/philanthropy_valuesbased_investments/indian-philanthrophy.pdf
18. *Harijan* (newspaper) 1 Feb 1942. **Recited from** Sundar, Pushpa. "Philanthropy in the Building of Modern India." *Revealing Indian Philanthropy*. Eds. Mathieu Cantegreil, Dweep Chanana, and Ruth Kattumuri. London, United Kingdom: Alliance Publishing Trust, 2013, 31–43. Web. 20 Apr. 2017. https://www.ubs.com/content/dam/ubs/global/wealth_management/philanthropy_valuesbased_investments/indian-philanthrophy.pdf
19. Sundar, Pushpa. "Philanthropy in the Building of Modern India." *Revealing Indian Philanthropy*. Eds. Mathieu Cantegreil, Dweep Chanana, and Ruth Kattumuri. London, United Kingdom: Alliance Publishing Trust, 2013, 31–43. Web. 20 Apr. 2017. https://www.ubs.com/content/dam/ubs/global/wealth_management/philanthropy_valuesbased_investments/indian-philanthrophy.pdf
20. Cantegreil, Mathieu, Dweep Chanana, and Ruth Kattumuri, eds. *Revealing Indian Philanthropy*. London, United Kingdom: Alliance Publishing Trust, 2013. Web. 20 Apr. 2017. https://www.ubs.com/content/dam/ubs/global/wealth_management/philanthropy_valuesbased_investments/indian-philanthrophy.pdf

21. "Overview of Civil Society Organizations: India." (n.d.): n. pag. *Civil Society Briefs*. Asian Development Bank, June 2009. Web. 20 Apr. 2017. https://www.adb.org/sites/default/files/publication/28966/csb-ind.pdf
22. Sundar, Pushpa. "Philanthropy in the Building of Modern India." *Revealing Indian Philanthropy*. Eds. Mathieu Cantegreil, Dweep Chanana, and Ruth Kattumuri. London, United Kingdom: Alliance Publishing Trust, 2013, 31–43. Web. 20 Apr. 2017. https://www.ubs.com/content/dam/ubs/global/wealth_management/philanthropy_valuesbased_investments/indian-philanthrophy.pdf
23. Mohan, Sudha. "Role and Relevance of Civil Society Organisations." *The Indian Journal of Political Science* 63.2/3 (2002): 193–211. *JSTOR*. Web. 20 Apr. 2017. http://www.jstor.org/stable/10.2307/42753686?ref=search-gateway:c88f1a7d1e26e6da0350cd681c7fd3e4
24. Sheth, Arpan, Dinkar Ayilavarapu, and Anant Bhagwati. *India Philanthropy Report 2015: Accelerating the Next Philanthropic Wave*. Rep. Bain & Company, 21 Mar. 2015. Web. 20 Apr. 2017. http://www.bain.com/Images/BAIN_REPORT_India_Philanthropy_Report_2015.pdf
25. Sheth, Arpan, Dinkar Ayilavarapu, and Anant Bhagwati. *India Philanthropy Report 2015: Accelerating the Next Philanthropic Wave*. Rep. Bain & Company, 21 Mar. 2015. Web. 20 Apr. 2017. http://www.bain.com/Images/BAIN_REPORT_India_Philanthropy_Report_2015.pdf
26. Sheth, Arpan, Deval Sanghavi, Anant Bhagwati, Srikrishnan Srinivasan, and Pakzan Dastoor. *India Philanthropy Report 2017: The Individual Philanthropist's Path to Full Potential*. Rep. Bain & company and Dasra, 4 Mar. 2017. Web. 20 Apr. 2017. http://www.bain.com/Images/REPORT_India_Philanthropy_2017.pdf
27. Bankoff, Greg. "Dangers to Going It Alone: Social Capital and the Origins of Community Resilience in the Philippines." *Continuity and Change* 22.02 (2007): 327–55. Web. 27 Mar. 2017.
28. Bankoff, Greg. "Dangers to Going It Alone: Social Capital and the Origins of Community Resilience in the Philippines." *Continuity and Change* 22.02 (2007): 327–55. Web. 27 Mar. 2017.
29. Velasco, Gisela. "Corporate Philanthropy in Asia: The Philippine Case: An Overview of East and Southeast Asian Philanthropy." Center on Philanthropy and Civil Society, n.d. Web. 27 Mar. 2017. http://www.philanthropy.org/publications/online_publications/asia.pdf
30. "Civil Society in the Philippines." (n.d.): n. pag. *Civil Society Briefs*. Asian Development Bank, Feb. 2013. Web. 27 Mar. 2017.
31. Bankoff, Greg. "Dangers to Going It Alone: Social capital and the Origins of Community Resilience in the Philippines." *Continuity and Change*, 22.02 (2007): 327–55. Web. 27 Mar. 2017.

32. "Civil Society in the Philippines." (n.d.): n. pag. *Civil Society Briefs*. Asian Development Bank, Feb. 2013. Web. 27 Mar. 2017.
33. Ferrer, Miriam Coronel. "The Philippine State and Civil Society Discourse and Praxis." *Korea Observer*, 35.3 (2004): 535–71. Web. 27 Mar. 2017.
34. "Civil Society in the Philippines." (n.d.): n. pag. *Civil Society Briefs*. Asian Development Bank, Feb. 2013. Web. 27 Mar. 2017.
35. Ferrer, Miriam Coronel. "The Philippine State and Civil Society Discourse and Praxis." *Korea Observer*, 35.3 (2004): 535–71. Web. 27 Mar. 2017.
36. Bankoff, Greg. "Dangers to Going It Alone: Social capital and the Origins of Community Resilience in the Philippines." *Continuity and Change*, 22.02 (2007): 327–55. Web. 27 Mar. 2017.
37. "Civil Society in the Philippines." (n.d.): n. pag. *Civil Society Briefs*. Asian Development Bank, Feb. 2013. Web. 27 Mar. 2017.
38. Velasco, Gisela. "Corporate Philanthropy in Asia: The Philippine Case: An Overview of East and Southeast Asian Philanthropy." Center on Philanthropy and Civil Society, n.d. Web. 27 Mar. 2017. http://www.philanthropy.org/publications/online_publications/asia.pdf
39. Bankoff, Greg. "Dangers to Going It Alone: Social capital and the Origins of Community Resilience in the Philippines." *Continuity and Change*, 22.02 (2007): 327–55. Web. 27 Mar. 2017.
40. Eaton, Kent. "Restoration or Transformation? *Trapos* versus NGOs in the Democratization of the Philippines." *The Journal of Asian Studies*, 62.02 (2003): 469–96. Web.
41. "Civil Society in the Philippines." (n.d.): n. pag. *Civil Society Briefs*. Asian Development Bank, Feb. 2013. Web. 27 Mar. 2017.
42. Eaton, Kent. "Restoration or Transformation? *Trapos* versus NGOs in the Democratization of the Philippines." *The Journal of Asian Studies*, 62.02 (2003): 469–96. Web.
43. Magadia, José. "Contemporary Civil society in the Philippines." *Southeast Asian Affairs* (1999): 253–68. *JSTOR*. Web. 27 Mar. 2017. http://www.jstor.org/stable/10.2307/27912230?ref=search-gateway:c5e364935963c99ae235b5ac9bfd44cb
44. Magadia, José. "Contemporary Civil Society in the Philippines." *Southeast Asian Affairs* (1999): 253–68. *JSTOR*. Web. 27 Mar. 2017. http://www.jstor.org/stable/10.2307/27912230?ref=search-gateway:c5e364935963c99ae235b5ac9bfd44cb
45. "2016 Social Progress Index | Social Progress Imperative." *Social Progress Imperative*. Social Progress Imperative, n.d. Web. 27 Mar. 2017. http://www.socialprogressimperative.org/global-index/#performance/countries/spi/dim1,dim2,dim3
46. "Table of Results: Corruption Perceptions Index 2015." *Transparency International*. Transparency International, n.d. Web. 27 Mar. 2017. http://www.transparency.org/cpi2015#results-table

47. Koo, Hagen. "Civil Society and Democracy in South Korea." *The Good Society*, 11.2 (2002): 40–45. *JSTOR*. Web. 10 Mar. 2017. http://www.jstor.org/stable/10.2307/20711071?ref=search-gateway:a3f5c24ae5874934fdc5fcf34d4fee3f
48. Kim, C. S. (1992). *The Culture of Korean Industry*, University of Arizona Press, Tucson. **Recited from** Bidet, Eric. "Explaining the Third Sector in South Korea." *Voluntas: International Journal of Voluntary and Nonprofit Organizations*, 13.2, Focus on Asia (2002): 131–47. *JSTOR*. Web. 10 Mar. 2017. http://www.jstor.org/stable/10.2307/27927772?ref=search-gateway:272a6845e8d68a2e3f641b31f730665d
49. Koo, Jeong-Woo. "The Origins of the Public Sphere and Civil Society: Private Academies and Petitions in Korea, 1506–1800." *Social Science History*, 31.3 (2007): 381–409. *JSTOR*. Web. 10 Mar. 2017. http://www.jstor.org/stable/10.2307/40267945?ref=search-gateway:5057ec42f7b174511ae513b459b7a38f
50. Koo, Jeong-Woo. "The Origins of the Public Sphere and Civil Society: Private Academies and Petitions in Korea, 1506–1800." *Social Science History*, 31.3 (2007): 381–409. *JSTOR*. Web. 10 Mar. 2017. http://www.jstor.org/stable/10.2307/40267945?ref=search-gateway:5057ec42f7b174511ae513b459b7a38f
51. Koo, Jeong-Woo. "The Origins of the Public Sphere and Civil Society: Private Academies and Petitions in Korea, 1506–1800." *Social Science History*, 31.3 (2007): 381–409. *JSTOR*. Web. 10 Mar. 2017. http://www.jstor.org/stable/10.2307/40267945?ref=search-gateway:5057ec42f7b174511ae513b459b7a38f.
52. Kim, Ho-Ki. "The State and Civil Society in South Korea, 1987–1999: CIVIL Movements and Democratic Consolidation." *Asian Perspective*, 25.1, Special Issue in Commemoration of the 25th Anniversary of Asian Perpsective (2001): 229–48. *JSTOR*. Web. 10 Mar. 2017. http://www.jstor.org/stable/10.2307/42704305?ref=search-gateway:1fde29fbb6bde5b4033ec8c0b297e6ce
53. Sohn, Yu Jean. "The Institutional Context of Korean Philanthropy and the Role of Government and (Quasi-) Community Foundations." Diss. U of Southern California, 2014. Aug. 2014. Web. 15 Mar. 2017. https://research.beautifulfund.org/wp-content/uploads/1/cfile23.uf.220734395428C8B5336645.pdf
54. Kim, Ho-Ki. "The State and Civil Society in South Korea, 1987–1999: Civil Movements and Democratic Consolidation." *Asian Perspective*, 25.1, Special Issue in Commemoration of the 25th Anniversary of Asian Perpsective (2001): 229–48. *JSTOR*. Web. 10 Mar. 2017. http://www.jstor.org/stable/10.2307/42704305?ref=search-gateway:1fde29fbb6bde5b4033ec8c0b297e6ce

55. Bidet, Eric. "Explaining the Third Sector in South Korea." *Voluntas: International Journal of Voluntary and Nonprofit Organizations*, 13.2, Focus on Asia (2002): 131–47. *JSTOR*. Web. 10 Mar. 2017. http://www.jstor.org/stable/10.2307/27927772?ref=search-gateway:272a6845e8d68a2e3f641b31f730665d
56. Koo, Hagen. "Civil Society and Democracy in South Korea." *The Good Society*, 11.2 (2002): 40–45. *JSTOR*. Web. 10 Mar. 2017. http://www.jstor.org/stable/10.2307/20711071?ref=search-gateway:a3f5c24ae5874934fdc5fcf34d4fee3f
57. Bidet, Eric. "Explaining the Third Sector in South Korea." *Voluntas: International Journal of Voluntary and Nonprofit Organizations*, 13.2, Focus on Asia (2002): 131–47. *JSTOR*. Web. 10 Mar. 2017. http://www.jstor.org/stable/10.2307/27927772?ref=search-gateway:272a6845e8d68a2e3f641b31f730665d
58. Kim, Inchoon and Changsoon Hwang. "Defining the Nonprofit Sector: South Korea." *Working Papers of the Johns Hopkins Comparative Nonprofit Sector Project*, No. 41. Blatimore: The Johns Hopkins Center for Civil Society Studies, 2002.
59. Kim, Ho-Ki. "The State and Civil Society in South Korea, 1987–1999: Civil Movements and Democratic Consolidation." *Asian Perspective*, 25.1, Special Issue in Commemoration of the 25th Anniversary of Asian Perpsective (2001): 229–48. *JSTOR*. Web. 10 Mar. 2017. http://www.jstor.org/stable/10.2307/42704305?ref=search-gateway:1fde29fbb6bde5b4033ec8c0b297e6ce
60. Bruce Cumings, *The Origins of the Korean War: Liberation and the Emergence of Separate Regimes, 1945–47* (Princeton, NJ: Princeton University Press, 1981). **Recited from** Kim, Ho-Ki. "The State and Civil Society in South Korea, 1987–1999: Civil Movements and Democratic Consolidation." *Asian Perspective*, 25.1, Special Issue in Commemoration of the 25th Anniversary of Asian Perpsective (2001): 229–48. *JSTOR*. Web. 10 Mar. 2017. http://www.jstor.org/stable/10.2307/42704305?ref=search-gateway:1fde29fbb6bde5b4033ec8c0b297e6ce
61. Koo, Hagen. "Civil Society and Democracy in South Korea." *The Good Society*, 11.2 (2002): 40–45. *JSTOR*. Web. 10 Mar. 2017. http://www.jstor.org/stable/10.2307/20711071?ref=search-gateway:a3f5c24ae5874934fdc5fcf34d4fee3f
62. Bidet, Eric. "Explaining the Third Sector in South Korea." *Voluntas: International Journal of Voluntary and Nonprofit Organizations*, 13.2, Focus on Asia (2002): 131–47. *JSTOR*. Web. 10 Mar. 2017. http://www.jstor.org/stable/10.2307/27927772?ref=search-gateway:272a6845e8d68a2e3f641b31f730665d

63. Sohn, Yu Jean. "The Institutional Context of Korean Philanthropy and the Role of Government and (Quasi-) Community Foundations." Diss. U of Southern California, 2014. Aug. 2014. Web. 15 Mar. 2017. https://research.beautifulfund.org/wp-content/uploads/1/cfile23.uf.220734395428C8B5336645.pdf
64. *The Saemaul Undong Movement in the Republic of Korea: Sharing Knowledge on Community-driven Development*. Manila, Philippines: Asian Development Bank, 2012. Asian Development Bank, 2012. Web. 23 Mar. 2017. https://www.adb.org/sites/default/files/publication/29881/saemaul-undong-movement-korea.pdf
65. *The Saemaul Undong Movement in the Republic of Korea: Sharing Knowledge on Community-driven Development*. Manila, Philippines: Asian Development Bank, 2012. Asian Development Bank, 2012. Web. 23 Mar. 2017. https://www.adb.org/sites/default/files/publication/29881/saemaul-undong-movement-korea.pdf
66. Kim, Ho-Ki. "The State and Civil Society in South Korea, 1987–1999: Civil Movements and Democratic Consolidation." *Asian Perspective*, 25.1, Special Issue in Commemoration of the 25th Anniversary of Asian Perpsective (2001): 229–48. *JSTOR*. Web. 10 Mar. 2017. http://www.jstor.org/stable/10.2307/42704305?ref=search-gateway:1fde29fbb6bde5b4033ec8c0b297e6ce
67. Bidet, Eric. "Explaining the Third Sector in South Korea." *Voluntas: International Journal of Voluntary and Nonprofit Organizations*, 13.2. Focus on Asia (2002): 131–47. *JSTOR*. Web. 10 Mar. 2017. http://www.jstor.org/stable/10.2307/27927772?ref=search-gateway:272a6845e8d68a2e3f641b31f730665d
68. Sohn, Yu Jean. "The Institutional Context of Korean Philanthropy and the Role of Government and (Quasi-) Community Foundations." Diss. U of Southern California, 2014. Aug. 2014. Web. 15 Mar. 2017. https://research.beautifulfund.org/wp-content/uploads/1/cfile23.uf.220734395428C8B5336645.pdf
69. "Introduction to Confucian Thought." *Asia for Educators*. Columbia University, n.d. Web. 8 Mar. 2017. http://afe.easia.columbia.edu/special/china_1000bce_confucius_intro.htm
70. United Nations Development Programme, *Unleashing the Potential of Philanthropy in China*, 2015, p. 8.
71. Fuller, Pierre. "China's Charitable Past." *The New York Times*. The New York Times, 28 Sep. 2010. Web. 13 July 2016. http://www.nytimes.com/2010/09/29/opinion/29iht-edfuller.html
72. Qin, Hui. "Understanding China's Third Sector (SSIR)." Trans. Chengpang Lee. Eds. Chengpang Lee. Stanford Social Innovation Review, 16 Feb. 2017. Web. 1 Mar. 2017. https://ssir.org/articles/entry/understanding_chinas_third_sector

73. Johnson, Ian. "The Death and Life of China's Civil Society." *JSTOR [JSTOR]*. American Political Science Association, Sep. 2003. Web. 1 Mar. 2017. www.jstor.org/stable/3688711
74. United Nations Development Programme, *Unleashing the Potential of Philanthropy in China*, 2015, p. 8.
75. Qin, Hui. "Understanding China's Third Sector (SSIR)." Trans. Chengpang Lee. Ed. Chengpang Lee. Stanford Social Innovation Review, 16 Feb. 2017. Web. 1 Mar. 2017. https://ssir.org/articles/entry/understanding_chinas_third_sector
76. Zhuang, Ailing. "Building the Philanthropy Sector in China." *Zhen Zheng De Wen Ti Jie Jue Zhe: She Hui Qi Ye Ru He Yong Chuang Xin Gai Bian Shi Jie = The Real Problem Solvers*. By Ruth A. Shapiro. Trans. Ran Liu. Beijing: Zhong Guo Ren Min Da Xue Chu Ban She, 2014. N. pag. Print.
77. Qin, Hui. "Understanding China's Third Sector (SSIR)." Trans. Chengpang Lee. Ed. Chengpang Lee. Stanford Social Innovation Review, 16 Feb. 2017. Web. 1 Mar. 2017. https://ssir.org/articles/entry/understanding_chinas_third_sector
78. Wong, Sonia Man Lai. "Non-Governmental Organisations and Government in China: Enemies or Allies?" *Governing Society in Contemporary China*. Ed. Lijun Yang and Wei Shan. New Jersey: World Scientific, 2017, 70. Print.
79. Hong, Haolan, Michelle Phillips, Visqi He, and Jaime FlorCruz. "Red Cross China in Credibility Crisis." *CNN*. Cable News Network, 6 July 2011. Web. 8 Mar. 2017. http://edition.cnn.com/2011/WORLD/asiapcf/07/06/china.redcross/
80. Sun, Yuanqing. "Donations to Dropped 90% Due to Charity Trust Crisis." *China Daily Europe*. State Council Information Office, 26 Aug. 2011. Web. 8 Mar. 2017. http://europe.chinadaily.com.cn/china/2011-08/26/content_13200166.htm
81. Witt, Michael A., and Gordon Redding. "China: Authoritarian Capitalism." *The Oxford Handbook of Asian Business Systems*. Eds. Michael A. Witt and Gordon Redding. Oxford, United Kingdom: Oxford UP, 2015, 23. Print.
82. "WVS Database." *WVS Database*. World Values Survey Association, n.d. Web. 8 Mar. 2017. http://www.worldvaluessurvey.org/WVSOnline.jsp
83. "《慈善法》来了,公益的春大还会远吗?" 财新网. Ed. 和谦 徐. 财新网, 11 Mar. 2016. Web. 18 July 2016. http://topics.caixin.com/2016-03-11/100918963.html
84. "慈善法如何"善法更善":8大进步与10大期待." 财新网. Ed. 帆 张. 财新网, 9 Mar. 2016. Web. 18 July 2016. http://opinion.caixin.com/2016-03-09/100917992.html
85. United Nations Development Programme, *Unleashing the Potential of Philanthropy in China*, 2015, 21–22.

86. Chin, Josh. "The Good—And Bad—About China's New Charity Law." *The Wall Street Journal.* Dow Jones. 16 Mar. 2016. Web. 13 July 2016.
87. Peng, Jianmei. *China Charitable Giving Report.* China Charity Information Center, Beijing, China, 2014, p. 25.
88. Feng, Xiaoming. *China's Charitable Foundations: Development and Policy-Related Issues.* Stanford Center for International Development Working Paper No. 485, 2013.
89. Peng, Jianmei. *China Charitable Giving Report.* China Charity Information Center, Beijing, China, 2014, p. 25.
90. China Charitable Giving Report 2014, http://china.cnr.cn/ygxw/20150920/t20150920_519909785.shtml, and Liu, Zhongxiang *Annual Report on China's Foundation Development.* Beijing Social Sciences Academic Press, China, 2013.
91. Edmonds, Richard Louis, and Steven M. Goldstein. "Taiwan in the Twentieth Century: An Introduction." *The China Quarterly*, 165 (2001): n. pag. Web. 3 Apr. 2017.
92. Chu, R. L. "Charity and Altruistic Behaviour in Chinese Society." *Bulletin of the Institute of Ethnology Academia Sinica*, 75 (1993): 105–32. Web. 3 Apr. 2017. **Recited from** Pan, Chung-Dao. "Third Sector Organisations and Social Welfare: A Study of the Role of Social Service and Charitable Organisations in Taiwan." *Aston University Ph.D Thesis* (2007): 1–326. July 2007. Web. 3 Apr. 2017.
93. Ting, J. C. "Merit-Accumulation Behaviour in Cultural Context: An Example from Participants in Taiwan's Buddhist Tzu-Chi Association, with Implications for Cross-Cultural Studies on Helping Behaviour." *Bulletin of the Institute of Ethnology Academia Sinica*, 85 (1998): 113–77. Web. 3 Apr. 2017. **Recited from** Pan, Chung-Dao. "Third Sector Organisations and Social Welfare: A Study of the Role of Social Service and Charitable Organisations in Taiwan." *Aston University Ph.D Thesis* (2007): 1–326. July 2007. Web. 3 Apr. 2017.
94. Hsu, Elizabeth. "Apple Daily: Why Tzu Chi Is Sparking Resentment." *Taiwan News*, 6 Mar. 2015. Web. 9 Apr. 2017. http://www.taiwannews.com.tw/en/news/2698712
95. Pan, Chung-Dao. "Third Sector Organisations and Social Welfare: A Study of the Role of Social Service and Charitable Organisations in Taiwan." *Aston University Ph.D Thesis* (2007): 1–326. July 2007. Web. 3 Apr. 2017.
96. Hsiao, Hsin-Huang Michael. "Emerging Social Movements and the Rise of a Demanding Civil Society in Taiwan." *The Australian Journal of Chinese Affairs*, 24 (1990): 163–80. *JSTOR*. Web. 3 Apr. 2017. http://www.jstor.org/stable/10.2307/2158893?ref=search-gateway:7c7d155863a7250fbdcefe77680e4223

97. Hsiao, Hsin-Huang Michael. "Emerging Social Movements and the Rise of a Demanding Civil Society in Taiwan." *The Australian Journal of Chinese Affairs*, 24 (1990): 163–80. *JSTOR*. Web. 3 Apr. 2017. http://www.jstor.org/stable/10.2307/2158893?ref=search-gateway:7c7d155863a7250fbdcefe77680e4223
98. Hsiao, Hsin-Huang Michael. "Emerging Social Movements and the Rise of a Demanding Civil Society in Taiwan." *The Australian Journal of Chinese Affairs*, 24 (1990): 163–80. *JSTOR*. Web. 3 Apr. 2017. http://www.jstor.org/stable/10.2307/2158893?ref=search-gateway:7c7d155863a7250fbdcefe77680e4223
99. Hsiao, Hsin-Huang Michael. "Emerging Social Movements and the Rise of a Demanding Civil Society in Taiwan." *The Australian Journal of Chinese Affairs*, 24 (1990): 163–80. *JSTOR*. Web. 3 Apr. 2017. http://www.jstor.org/stable/10.2307/2158893?ref=search-gateway:7c7d155863a7250fbdcefe77680e4223
100. Hsiao, Hsin-Huang Michael. "Emerging Social Movements and the Rise of a Demanding Civil Society in Taiwan." *The Australian Journal of Chinese Affairs*, 24 (1990): 163–80. *JSTOR*. Web. 3 Apr. 2017. http://www.jstor.org/stable/10.2307/2158893?ref=search-gateway:7c7d155863a7250fbdcefe77680e4223
101. Jung, Jai Kwan. "Popular Mobilization and Democratization: A Comparative Study of South Korea and Taiwan." *Korea Observer*, 42.3 (2011): 377–411. Web. 3 Apr. 2017.
102. Jung, Jai Kwan. "Popular Mobilization and Democratization: A Comparative Study of South Korea and Taiwan." *Korea Observer*, 42.3 (2011): 377–411. Web. 3 Apr. 2017.
103. Tien, Hung-mao. "Taiwan's Evolution toward Democracy: A Historical Perspective." *Taiwan: Beyond the Economic Miracle*. Ed. Denis Fred Simon and Michael Y. M. Kau. Armonk, NY: M.E. Sharpe, 1997. N. pag. Print.
104. Hsu, Carolyn, Fang-Yu Chen, Jamie P. Horsley, and Rachel Stern. "The State of NGOs in China Today." *Brookings*. Brookings Institution, 1 Feb. 2017. Web. 3 Apr. 2017. https://www.brookings.edu/blog/up-front/2016/12/15/the-state-of-ngos-in-china-today/
105. Lee, Wei-chin. "Diplomatic Impetus and Altruistic Impulse: NGOs and the Expansion of Taiwan's International Space." *Brookings*. Brookings Institution, 28 July 2016. Web. 3 Apr. 2017. https://www.brookings.edu/opinions/diplomatic-impetus-and-altruistic-impulse-ngos-and-the-expansion-of-taiwans-international-space/
106. *Statistical Yearbook of Interior*. Ministry of the Interior, n.d. Web. 3 Apr. 2017. http://sowf.moi.gov.tw/stat/year/elist.htm#4+Cooperative+&+Civil+Associations

107. Hirata, Keiko. "Civil Society and NGOs in Japan." *Civil Society in Japan: The Growing Role of NGOs in Tokyo's Aid and Development Policy*. By Keiko Hirata. Basingstoke: Palgrave Macmillan, 2002, 8–49. Web. 2 May 2017. http://www.csun.edu/~kh246690/civil_society_ch1.pdf
108. Kawashima, Nobuko. "The Emerging Voluntary Sector in Japan: Issues and Prospects." (1999): 1–48. London School of Economics and Political Science, Centre for Voluntary Organisation. Web. 2 May 2017. http://eprints.lse.ac.uk/29095/1/IWP7nobuko.pdf
109. Amenomori, Takayoshi. "Defining the Nonprofit Sector: Japan." *Working Papers of the John Hopkings Comparative Nonprofit Sector Project*, No. 15. Ed. L. M. Salamon and H. K. Anheier. Baltimore: The Johns Hopkins Institute for Policy Studies, 1993. Web. 2 May 2017. http://ccss.jhu.edu/wp-content/uploads/downloads/2011/09/Japan_CNP_WP15_1993.pdf
110. Amenomori, Takayoshi. "Defining the Nonprofit Sector: Japan." *Working Papers of the John Hopkins Comparative Nonprofit Sector Project*, No. 15. Ed. L. M. Salamon and H. K. Anheier. Baltimore: The Johns Hopkins Institute for Policy Studies, 1993. Web. 2 May 2017. http://ccss.jhu.edu/wp-content/uploads/downloads/2011/09/Japan_CNP_WP15_1993.pdf
111. Yamamoto, Tadashi. "The Nonprofit Sector in Japan: Historical Evolution and Future Challenges." *The Johns Hopkins Comparative Nonprofit Sector Project* (1998): 84–105. *Japan Center for International Exchange*. The Johns Hopkins Institute for Policy Studies. Web. 2 May 2017. http://www.jcie.org/researchpdfs/Role_Nonstate/6_Chapter%205.pdf
112. Amenomori, Takayoshi. "Defining the Nonprofit Sector: Japan." *Working Papers of the John Hopkins Comparative Nonprofit Sector Project*, No. 15. Eds. L. M. Salamon and H. K. Anheier. Baltimore: The Johns Hopkins Institute for Policy Studies, 1993. Web. 2 May 2017. http://ccss.jhu.edu/wp-content/uploads/downloads/2011/09/Japan_CNP_WP15_1993.pdf
113. Yamamoto, Tadashi. "The Nonprofit Sector in Japan: Historical Evolution and Future Challenges." *The Johns Hopkins Comparative Nonprofit Sector Project* (1998): 84–105. *Japan Center for International Exchange*. The Johns Hopkins Institute for Policy Studies. Web. 2 May 2017. http://www.jcie.org/researchpdfs/Role_Nonstate/6_Chapter%205.pdf
114. Amenomori, Takayoshi. "Defining the Nonprofit Sector: Japan." *Working Papers of the John Hopkins Comparative Nonprofit Sector Project*, No. 15. Ed. L. M. Salamon and H. K. Anheier. Baltimore: The Johns Hopkins Institute for Policy Studies, 1993. Web. 2 May 2017. http://ccss.jhu.edu/wp-content/uploads/downloads/2011/09/Japan_CNP_WP15_1993.pdf

115. Yamamoto, Tadashi. "The Nonprofit Sector in Japan: Historical Evolution and Future Challenges." *The Johns Hopkins Comparative Nonprofit Sector Project* (1998): 84–105. *Japan Center for International Exchange*. The Johns Hopkins Institute for Policy Studies. Web. 2 May 2017. http://www.jcie.org/researchpdfs/Role_Nonstate/6_Chapter%205.pdf
116. Amenomori, Takayoshi. "Defining the Nonprofit Sector: Japan." *Working Papers of the John Hopkins Comparative Nonprofit Sector Project*, No. 15. Ed. L. M. Salamon and H. K. Anheier. Baltimore: The Johns Hopkins Institute for Policy Studies, 1993. Web. 2 May 2017. http://ccss.jhu.edu/wp-content/uploads/downloads/2011/09/Japan_CNP_WP15_1993.pdf
117. Kawashima, Nobuko. "The Emerging Voluntary Sector in Japan: Issues and Prospects." (1999): 1–48. London School of Economics and Political Science, Centre for Voluntary Organisation. Web. 2 May 2017. http://eprints.lse.ac.uk/29095/1/IWP7nobuko.pdf
118. Pekkanen, Robert. "After the Developmental State: Civil Society in Japan." *Journal of East Asian Studies*, 4.3, SPECIAL ISSUE: After the Developmental State in East Asia? (2004): 363–88. *JSTOR*. Web. 2 May 2017. http://www.jstor.org/stable/10.2307/23417947?ref=search-gateway:e128523bbc7e6d0ed972605e0f0a5b51
119. Kawashima, Nobuko. "The Emerging Voluntary Sector in Japan: Issues and Prospects." (1999): 1–48. London School of Economics and Political Science, Centre for Voluntary Organisation. Web. 2 May 2017. http://eprints.lse.ac.uk/29095/1/IWP7nobuko.pdf
120. Hirata, Keiko. "Civil Society and NGOs in Japan." *Civil Society in Japan: The Growing Role of NGOs in Tokyo's Aid and Development Policy*. By Keiko Hirata. Basingstoke: Palgrave Macmillan, 2002, 8–49. Web. 2 May 2017. http://www.csun.edu/~kh246690/civil_society_ch1.pdf
121. Hirata, Keiko. "Civil Society and NGOs in Japan." *Civil Society in Japan: The Growing Role of NGOs in Tokyo's Aid and Development Policy*. By Keiko Hirata. Basingstoke: Palgrave Macmillan, 2002, 8–49. Web. 2 May 2017. http://www.csun.edu/~kh246690/civil_society_ch1.pdf
122. Hirata, Keiko. "Civil Society and NGOs in Japan." *Civil Society in Japan: The Growing Role of NGOs in Tokyo's Aid and Development Policy*. By Keiko Hirata. Basingstoke: Palgrave Macmillan, 2002, 8–49. Web. 2 May 2017. http://www.csun.edu/~kh246690/civil_society_ch1.pdf
123. Pekkanen, Robert. "After the Developmental State: Civil Society in Japan." *Journal of East Asian Studies*, 4.3, SPECIAL ISSUE: After the Developmental State in East Asia? (2004): 363–88. *JSTOR*. Web. 2 May 2017. http://www.jstor.org/stable/10.2307/23417947?ref=search-gateway:e128523bbc7e6d0ed972605e0f0a5b51
124. Pekkanen, Robert. "After the Developmental State: Civil Society in Japan." *Journal of East Asian Studies*, 4.3, SPECIAL ISSUE: After the

Developmental State in East Asia? (2004): 363–88. *JSTOR*. Web. 2 May 2017. http://www.jstor.org/stable/10.2307/23417947?ref=search-gateway:e128523bbc7e6d0ed972605e0f0a5b51

125. Leng, Rachel. "Japan's Civil Society from Kobe to Tohoku: Impact of Policy Changes on Government-NGO Relationship and Effectiveness of Post-Disaster Relief." *Electronic Journal of Contemporary Japanese Studies*, 15.1 (2015): n. pag. 19 Apr. 2015. Web. 2 May 2017. http://scholar.harvard.edu/files/rachel_leng/files-ejcjs_-_japans_civil_society_from_kobe_to_tohoku_rachel_leng.pdf
126. Leng, Rachel. "Japan's Civil Society from Kobe to Tohoku: Impact of Policy Changes on Government-NGO Relationship and Effectiveness of Post-Disaster Relief." *Electronic Journal of Contemporary Japanese Studies*, 15.1 (2015): n. pag. 19 Apr. 2015. Web. 2 May 2017. http://scholar.harvard.edu/files/rachel_leng/files-ejcjs_-_japans_civil_society_from_kobe_to_tohoku_rachel_leng.pdf
127. Leng, Rachel. "Japan's Civil Society from Kobe to Tohoku: Impact of Policy Changes on Government-NGO Relationship and Effectiveness of Post-Disaster Relief." *Electronic Journal of Contemporary Japanese Studies*, 15.1 (2015): n. pag. 19 Apr. 2015. Web. 2 May 2017. http://scholar.harvard.edu/files/rachel_leng/files-ejcjs_-_japans_civil_society_from_kobe_to_tohoku_rachel_leng.pdf
128. Leng, Rachel. "Japan's Civil Society from Kobe to Tohoku: Impact of Policy Changes on Government-NGO Relationship and Effectiveness of Post-Disaster Relief." *Electronic Journal of Contemporary Japanese Studies*, 15.1 (2015): n. pag. 19 Apr. 2015. Web. 2 May 2017. http://scholar.harvard.edu/files/rachel_leng/files-ejcjs_-_japans_civil_society_from_kobe_to_tohoku_rachel_leng.pdf
129. Pekkanen, Robert. "After the Developmental State: Civil Society in Japan." *Journal of East Asian Studies*, 4.3, SPECIAL ISSUE: After the Developmental State in East Asia? (2004): 363–88. *JSTOR*. Web. 2 May 2017. http://www.jstor.org/stable/10.2307/23417947?ref=search-gateway:e128523bbc7e6d0ed972605e0f0a5b51
130. Pekkanen, Robert. "After the Developmental State: Civil Society in Japan." *Journal of East Asian Studies*, 4.3, SPECIAL ISSUE: After the Developmental State in East Asia? (2004): 363–88. *JSTOR*. Web. 2 May 2017. http://www.jstor.org/stable/10.2307/23417947?ref=search-gateway:e128523bbc7e6d0ed972605e0f0a5b51
131. "GDP per capita (current US$)." *The World Bank DataBank*. The World Bank, n.d. Web. 19 Oct. 2016. http://data.worldbank.org/indicator/NY.GDP.PCAP.CD
132. "Life Expectancy at Birth, Total (years)." *The World Bank DataBank*. The World Bank, n.d. Web. 19 Oct. 2016. http://data.worldbank.org/indicator/SP.DYN.LE00.IN

133. "Latest Data | Department of Statistics Singapore." *Department of Statistics Singapore*. Government of Singapore, n.d. Web. 19 Oct. 2016. http://www.singstat.gov.sg/statistics/latest-data
134. "Singapore Philanthropy Findings." *Singapore Philanthropy Findings*. Coutts, n.d. Web. 19 Oct. 2016. http://philanthropy.coutts.com/en/reports/2015/singapore/findings.html
135. "Singapore Philanthropy Discussion." *Singapore Philanthropy Discussion*. Coutts, n.d. Web. 19 Oct. 2016. http://philanthropy.coutts.com/en/reports/2015/singapore/discussion.html
136. "Singapore Philanthropy Discussion." *Singapore Philanthropy Discussion*. Coutts, n.d. Web. 19 Oct. 2016. http://philanthropy.coutts.com/en/reports/2015/singapore/discussion.html
137. Chong, Terence. "Civil Society in Singapore: Popular Discourses and Concepts." *Sojourn: Journal of Social Issues in Southeast Asia*, 20.2, Democracy and Civil Society: NGO Politics in Singapore (2005): 273–301. *JSTOR*. Web. 15 May 2017. http://www.jstor.org/stable/10.2307/41308060?ref=search-gateway:4ec2b7eaa9a02883058877fb265445fe
138. Ho, Khai Leong. "Review: *Singapore Civil Society and British Power* by E. Kay Gillis." *Sojourn: Journal of Social Issues in Southeast Asia*, 21.2, Dynamics of the Local (2006): 271–74. *JSTOR*. Web. 15 May 2017. http://www.jstor.org/stable/10.2307/41308079?ref=search-gateway:be59c93dbb0f7c2f7f92fe4de9885fe5
139. Tay, Simon S. C. "Towards a Singaporean Civil Society." *Southeast Asian Affairs* (1998): 244–61. *JSTOR*. Web. 15 May 2017. http://www.jstor.org/stable/10.2307/27912207?ref=search-gateway:939d64b148afad72570745020c95ceb0
140. Chong, Terence. "Civil Society in Singapore: Popular Discourses and Concepts." *Sojourn: Journal of Social Issues in Southeast Asia*, 20.2, Democracy and Civil Society: NGO Politics in Singapore (2005): 273–301. *JSTOR*. Web. 15 May 2017. http://www.jstor.org/stable/10.2307/41308060?ref=search-gateway:4ec2b7eaa9a02883058877fb265445fe
141. Tay, Simon S. C. "Towards a Singaporean Civil Society." *Southeast Asian Affairs* (1998): 244–61. *JSTOR*. Web. 15 May 2017. http://www.jstor.org/stable/10.2307/27912207?ref=search-gateway:939d64b148afad72570745020c95ceb0
142. Chong, Terence. "Civil Society in Singapore: Popular Discourses and Concepts." *Sojourn: Journal of Social Issues in Southeast Asia*, 20.2, Democracy and Civil Society: NGO Politics in Singapore (2005): 273–301. *JSTOR*. Web. 15 May 2017. http://www.jstor.org/stable/10.2307/41308060?ref=search-gateway:4ec2b7eaa9a02883058877fb265445fe

143. Tay, Simon S. C. "Towards a Singaporean Civil Society." *Southeast Asian Affairs* (1998): 244–61. *JSTOR*. Web. 15 May 2017. http://www.jstor.org/stable/10.2307/27912207?ref=search-gateway:939d64b148afad72570745020c95ceb0
144. Ortmann, Stephan. "Political Change and Civil Society Coalitions in Singapore." *Government and Opposition*, 50.1 (2015): 119–39. Web.
145. Tay, Simon S. C. "Towards a Singaporean Civil Society." *Southeast Asian Affairs* (1998): 244–61. *JSTOR*. Web. 15 May 2017. http://www.jstor.org/stable/10.2307/27912207?ref=search-gateway:939d64b148afad72570745020c95ceb0
146. Tay, Simon S. C. "Towards a Singaporean Civil Society." *Southeast Asian Affairs* (1998): 244–61. *JSTOR*. Web. 15 May 2017. http://www.jstor.org/stable/10.2307/27912207?ref=search-gateway:939d64b148afad72570745020c95ceb0
147. Lee, Terence. "Gestural Politics: Civil Society in "New" Singapore." *Sojourn: Journal of Social Issues in Southeast Asia*, 20.2, Democracy and Civil Society: NGO Politics in Singapore (2005): 132–54. *JSTOR*. Web. 15 May 2017. http://www.jstor.org/stable/10.2307/41308055?ref=search-gateway:0c41f47c1b40c633d664338b56fefcf7
148. Ortmann, Stephan. "Political Change and Civil Society Coalitions in Singapore." *Government and Opposition*, 50.1 (2015): 119–39. Web.
149. Lee, Terence. "Gestural Politics: Civil Society in "New" Singapore." *Sojourn: Journal of Social Issues in Southeast Asia*, 20.2, Democracy and Civil Society: NGO Politics in Singapore (2005): 132–54. *JSTOR*. Web. 15 May 2017. http://www.jstor.org/stable/10.2307/41308055?ref=search-gateway:0c41f47c1b40c633d664338b56fefcf7
150. Lee, Terence. "Gestural Politics: Civil Society in 'New' Singapore." *Sojourn: Journal of Social Issues in Southeast Asia*, 20.2, Democracy and Civil Society: NGO Politics in Singapore (2005): 132–54. *JSTOR*. Web. 15 May 2017. http://www.jstor.org/stable/10.2307/41308055?ref=search-gateway:0c41f47c1b40c633d664338b56fefcf7
151. Ortmann, Stephan. "Political Change and Civil Society Coalitions in Singapore." *Government and Opposition*, 50.1 (2015): 119–39. Web.
152. Lee, Terence. "Gestural Politics: Civil Society in 'New' Singapore." *Sojourn: Journal of Social Issues in Southeast Asia*, 20.2, Democracy and Civil Society: NGO Politics in Singapore (2005): 132–54. *JSTOR*. Web. 15 May 2017. http://www.jstor.org/stable/10.2307/41308055?ref=search-gateway:0c41f47c1b40c633d664338b56fefcf7
153. Tay, Simon S. C. "Towards a Singaporean Civil Society." *Southeast Asian Affairs* (1998): 244–61. *JSTOR*. Web. 15 May 2017. http://www.jstor.org/stable/10.2307/27912207?ref=search-gateway:939d64b148afad72570745020c95ceb0

154. Tay, Simon S. C. "Towards a Singaporean Civil Society." *Southeast Asian Affairs* (1998): 244–61. *JSTOR*. Web. 15 May 2017. http://www.jstor.org/stable/10.2307/27912207?ref=search-gateway:939d64b148afad72570745020c95ceb0
155. Tay, Simon S. C. "Towards a Singaporean Civil Society." *Southeast Asian Affairs* (1998): 244–61. *JSTOR*. Web. 15 May 2017. http://www.jstor.org/stable/10.2307/27912207?ref=search-gateway:939d64b148afad72570745020c95ceb0
156. Chew, Hui Min. "Singapore Budget 2015: Tax Deduction of 200 per Cent the Amount Donated in Jubilee Year." *The Straits Times*. The Straits Times, 19 Jan. 2016. Web. 15 May 2017. http://www.straitstimes.com/singapore/singapore-budget-2015-tax-deduction-of-300-per-cent-the-amount-donated-in-jubilee-year
157. Goy, Priscilla. "Giving Week Gets 24% More Donations in Its Latest Collection." *The Straits Times*. The Straits Times, 19 Jan. 2016. Web. 15 May 2017. http://www.straitstimes.com/singapore/giving-week-gets-24-more-donations-in-its-latest-collection.
158. Fichtl, Eric. "An Introduction to the Third Sector in Hong Kong: Historical Developments and Current Outlook." (2006): 1–16. Web. 25 May 2017. http://www.ericfichtl.org/images/uploads/Fichtl_ThirdSectorHongKong.pdf
159. "Content & Overview." *Study on the Third Sector Landscape in Hong Kong* (2004): 1–37. *Research Reports—Archives*. Central Policy Unit—The Government of the Hong Kong Special Administrative Region, 27 Aug. 2004. Web. 25 May 2017. http://www.cpu.gov.hk/doc/en/research-reports/3rd_content.pdf
160. Lam, Wai-Fung, and James L. Perry. "The Role of the Nonprofit Sector in Hong Kong's Development." *Voluntas: International Journal of Voluntary and Nonprofit Organizations*, 11.4 (2000): 355–73. *JSTOR*. Web. 25 May 2017. http://www.jstor.org/stable/10.2307/27927698?ref=search-gateway:c42424e81b95082f47d8a77c36ffeb0f
161. "Content & Overview." *Study on the Third Sector Landscape in Hong Kong* (2004): 1–37. *Research Reports—Archives*. Central Policy Unit—The Government of the Hong Kong Special Administrative Region, 27 Aug. 2004. Web. 25 May 2017. http://www.cpu.gov.hk/doc/en/research-reports/3rd_content.pdf
162. Fichtl, Eric. "An Introduction to the Third Sector in Hong Kong: Historical Developments and Current Outlook." (2006): 1–16. Web. 25 May 2017. http://www.ericfichtl.org/images/uploads/Fichtl_ThirdSectorHongKong.pdf
163. "Content & Overview." *Study on the Third Sector Landscape in Hong Kong* (2004): 1–37. *Research Reports—Archives*. Central Policy Unit—The Government of the Hong Kong Special Administrative Region,

27 Aug. 2004. Web. 25 May 2017. http://www.cpu.gov.hk/doc/en/research-reports/3rd_content.pdf

164. Fichtl, Eric. "An Introduction to the Third Sector in Hong Kong: Historical Developments and Current Outlook." (2006): 1–16. Web. 25 May 2017. http://www.ericfichtl.org/images/uploads/Fichtl_ThirdSectorHongKong.pdf
165. "Content & Overview." *Study on the Third Sector Landscape in Hong Kong* (2004): 1–37. *Research Reports—Archives.* Central Policy Unit—The Government of the Hong Kong Special Administrative Region, 27 Aug. 2004. Web. 25 May 2017. http://www.cpu.gov.hk/doc/en/research-reports/3rd_content.pdf
166. "Content & Overview." *Study on the Third Sector Landscape in Hong Kong* (2004): 1–37. *Research Reports—Archives.* Central Policy Unit—The Government of the Hong Kong Special Administrative Region, 27 Aug. 2004. Web. 25 May 2017. http://www.cpu.gov.hk/doc/en/research-reports/3rd_content.pdf
167. "Hong Kong Philanthropy Findings." *Hong Kong Philanthropy Findings.* Coutts, n.d. Web. 19 Oct. 2016. http://philanthropy.coutts.com/en/reports/2015/hong-kong/findings.html
168. Fichtl, Eric. "An Introduction to the Third Sector in Hong Kong: Historical Developments and Current Outlook." (2006): 1–16. Web. 25 May 2017. http://www.ericfichtl.org/images/uploads/Fichtl_ThirdSectorHongKong.pdf
169. Lam, Wai-man, and Kay Chi-yan Lam. "China's United Front Work in Civil Society: The Case of Hong Kong." *International Journal of China Studies*, 4.3 (2013): 301–25. Web. 25 May 2017.
170. Hung, Ho-fung, and Iam-chong Ip. "Hong Kong's Democratic Movement and the Making of China's Offshore Civil Society." *Asian Survey*, 52.3 (2012): 504–27. *JSTOR*. Web. 25 May 2017. http://www.jstor.org/stable/10.1525/as.2012.52.3.504?ref=search-gateway:a33774b6e4eb71f0a11b50cca88d2ad4
171. Lam, Wai-Fung, and James L. Perry. "The Role of the Nonprofit Sector in Hong Kong's Development." *Voluntas: International Journal of Voluntary and Nonprofit Organizations*, 11.4 (2000): 355–73. *JSTOR*. Web. 25 May 2017. http://www.jstor.org/stable/10.2307/27927698?ref=search-gateway:c42424e81b95082f47d8a77c36ffeb0f
172. Loh, Christine. "Alive and Well but Frustrated: Hong Kong's Civil Society." *China Perspectives*, 2.70 (2007): 40–45. *JSTOR*. Web. 25 May 2017. http://www.jstor.org/stable/10.2307/24053505?ref=search-gateway:6edf9c50c962bb7551b555c32cdb4f1f
173. Sing, Ming. "Economic Development, Civil Society and Democratization in Hong Kong." *Journal of Contemporary Asia*, 26.4 (1996): 482–504. Web. 25 May 2017.

174. Chan, Ming K. "The Legacy of the British Administration of Hong Kong: A View from Hong Kong." *The China Quarterly*, 151 (1997): 567–82. *JSTOR*. Web. 25 May 2017. http://www.jstor.org/stable/10.2307/655254?ref=search-gateway:fc1a5427644c704230634 78ef3dda75f
175. Lam, Wai-Fung, and James L. Perry. "The Role of the Nonprofit Sector in Hong Kong's Development." *Voluntas: International Journal of Voluntary and Nonprofit Organizations*, 11.4 (2000): 355–73. *JSTOR*. Web. 25 May 2017. http://www.jstor.org/stable/10.2307/27927698?ref=search-gateway:c42424e81b95082f47d8a77c36ffeb0f
176. "Content & Overview." *Study on the Third Sector Landscape in Hong Kong* (2004): 1–37. *Research Reports—Archives*. Central Policy Unit—The Government of the Hong Kong Special Administrative Region, 27 Aug. 2004. Web. 25 May 2017. http://www.cpu.gov.hk/doc/en/research-reports/3rd_content.pdf
177. "Content & Overview." *Study on the Third Sector Landscape in Hong Kong* (2004): 1–37. *Research Reports—Archives*. Central Policy Unit—The Government of the Hong Kong Special Administrative Region, 27 Aug. 2004. Web. 25 May 2017. http://www.cpu.gov.hk/doc/en/research-reports/3rd_content.pdf
178. Pongsapich, Amara. "Politics of Civil Society." *Southeast Asian Affairs* (1999): 325–35. *JSTOR*. Web. 5 June 2017. http://www.jstor.org/stable/10.2307/27912234?ref=search-gateway:80fe3a074409cea3a124919 64379afef
179. Guruge, Ananda W. P., and G. D. Bond. "Generosity and Service in Theravada Buddhism." *Philanthropy in the World's Traditions*. Eds. Edward L. Queen II, Warren F. Ilchman, and Stanley N. Katz. N.p.: Indiana UP, 1998, 79–96. Print.
180. *Strengthening Philanthropy in the Asia Pacific: An Agenda for Action—Background Paper: Thailand*. Rep. Asia Pacific Philanthropy Consortium, July 2001. Web. 5 June 2017. http://unpan1.un.org/instradoc/groups/public/documents/APCITY/UNPAN005489.pdf
181. *Strengthening Philanthropy in the Asia Pacific: An Agenda for Action—Background Paper: Thailand*. Rep. Asia Pacific Philanthropy Consortium, July 2001. Web. 5 June 2017. http://unpan1.un.org/instradoc/groups/public/documents/APCITY/UNPAN005489.pdf
182. Ellington, John W., and Serene Chen. *The Thailand Report: National Landscape, Current Challenges and Opportunities for Growth*. Rep. Institute for Societal Leadership, Singapore Management University, n.d. Web. 5 June 2017. https://isl.smu.edu.sg/sites/default/files/isl_smu_edu_sg/CIL/Thailand%20CIR%20%28Final%20Draft%29.pdf
183. D. R. SarDesai, *Southeast Asia: Past & Present, Fifth Edition* (Boulder, CO: Westview Press, 2003), 139. **Recited from** Ellington, John W., and

Serene Chen. *The Thailand Report: National Landscape, Current Challenges and Opportunities for Growth.* Rep. Institute for Societal Leadership, Singapore Management University, n.d. Web. 5 June 2017. https://isl.smu.edu.sg/sites/default/files/isl_smu_edu_sg/CIL/Thailand%20CIR%20%28Final%20Draft%29.pdf

184. "Civil Society Briefs: Thailand." (n.d.): n. pag. *Civil Society Briefs.* Asian Development Bank. Nov. 2011. Web. 5 June 2017. https://www.adb.org/sites/default/files/publication/29149/csb-tha.pdf
185. Ellington, John W., and Serene Chen. *The Thailand Report: National Landscape, Current Challenges and Opportunities for Growth.* Rep. Institute for Societal Leadership, Singapore Management University, n.d. Web. 5 June 2017. https://isl.smu.edu.sg/sites/default/files/isl_smu_edu_sg/CIL/Thailand%20CIR%20%28Final%20Draft%29.pdf
186. Pongsapich, Amara. "Politics of Civil Society." *Southeast Asian Affairs* (1999): 325–35. *JSTOR*. Web. 5 June 2017. http://www.jstor.org/stable/10.2307/27912234?ref=search-gateway:80fe3a074409cea3a12491964379afef
187. Pongsapich, Amara. "Politics of Civil Society." *Southeast Asian Affairs* (1999): 325–35. *JSTOR*. Web. 5 June 2017. http://www.jstor.org/stable/10.2307/27912234?ref=search-gateway:80fe3a074409cea3a12491964379afef
188. Pongsapich, Amara. "Politics of Civil Society." *Southeast Asian Affairs* (1999): 325–35. *JSTOR*. Web. 5 June 2017. http://www.jstor.org/stable/10.2307/27912234?ref=search-gateway:80fe3a074409cea3a12491964379afef
189. Pathmanand, Ukrist. "Globalization and Democratic Development in Thailand: The New Path of the Military, Private Sector, and Civil Society." *Contemporary Southeast Asia*, 23.1 (2001): 24–42. *JSTOR*. Web. 5 June 2017. http://www.jstor.org/stable/10.2307/25798526?ref=search-gateway:80937643c2efd8f149173e50e1fb059e
190. "Civil Society Briefs: Thailand." (n.d.): n. pag. *Civil Society Briefs.* Asian Development Bank. Nov. 2011. Web. 5 June 2017. https://www.adb.org/sites/default/files/publication/29149/csb-tha.pdf
191. *Reflections on Thai Civil Society.* Rep. KEPA—Service Centre for Development Cooperation. Dec. 2011. Web. 5 June 2017. https://www.kepa.fi/tiedostot/reflections-on-thai-civil-society-2011.pdf
192. Pongsapich, Amara. "Politics of Civil Society." *Southeast Asian Affairs* (1999): 325–35. *JSTOR*. Web. 5 June 2017. http://www.jstor.org/stable/10.2307/27912234?ref=search-gateway:80fe3a074409cea3a12491964379afef
193. O'Neill, Jim. "Who You Calling a BRIC?" *Bloomberg View*. Bloomberg. 12 Nov. 2013. Web. 11 July 2017. https://www.bloomberg.com/view/articles/2013-11-12/who-you-calling-a-bric-

194. Ellington, John W. *The Indonesia Report: National Landscape, Current Challenges and Opportunities for Growth.* Rep. Institute for Societal Leadership, Singapore Management University, n.d. Web. 12 June 2017. http://isl.smu.edu.sg/sites/default/files/isl_smu_edu_sg/CIL/Indonesia%20CIR%20%208Final%20Draft%29.pdf
195. Osili, Una, and Çağla Ökten. "Giving in Indonesia: A Culture of Philanthropy Rooted in Islamic Tradition." *The Palgrave Handbook of Global Philanthropy.* Eds. Femida Handy and Pamala Wiepking. Basingstoke: Palgrave Macmillan, 2015, 388–403. Print.
196. *Strengthening Philanthropy in the Asia Pacific: An Agenda for Action—Background Paper: Indonesia.* Rep. Asia Pacific Philanthropy Consortium, July 2001. Web. 12 June 2017. http://unpan1.un.org/intradoc/groups/public/documents/apcity/unpan005484.pdf.
197. Osili, Una, and Çağla Ökten. "Giving in Indonesia: A Culture of Philanthropy Rooted in Islamic Tradition." *The Palgrave Handbook of Global Philanthropy.* Eds. Femida Handy and Pamala Wiepking. Basingstoke: Palgrave Macmillan, 2015, 388–403. Print.
198. *Strengthening Philanthropy in the Asia Pacific: An Agenda for Action—Background Paper: Indonesia.* Rep. Asia Pacific Philanthropy Consortium, July 2001. Web. 12 June 2017. http://unpan1.un.org/intradoc/groups/public/documents/apcity/unpan005484.pdf
199. Kloos, David. "Review: Faith and the State. A History of Islamic Philanthropy in Indonesia by Amelia Fauzia." *Bijdragen Tot De Taal-Land- En Volkenkunde,* 170.4, Colonial Re-Collections: Memories, Objects, and Performances (2014): 576–79. *JSTOR.* Web. 12 June 2017. http://www.jstor.org/stable/10.2307/43817977?ref=search-gateway:271a139c5808db8c6a9014c0683e223b
200. Fauzia, Amelia. "Faith and the State: A History of Islamic Philanthropy in Indonesia." Thesis. The University of Melbourne. 2008. Web. 12 June 2017. http://minerva-access.unimelb.edu.au/bitstream/handle/11343/35228/118527_amelia%20thesis.pdf?sequence=1
201. Osili, Una, and Çağla Ökten. "Giving in Indonesia: A Culture of Philanthropy Rooted in Islamic Tradition." *The Palgrave Handbook of Global Philanthropy.* Eds. Femida Handy and Pamala Wiepking. Basingstoke: Palgrave Macmillan, 2015, 388–403. Print.
202. Sakai, Minako. "Building a Partnership for Social Service Delivery in Indonesia: State and Faith-based Organisations." *Australian Journal of Social Issues,* 47.3 (2012): 373–88. *ProQuest.* Web. 12 June 2017.
203. Ellington, John W. *The Indonesia Report: National Landscape, Current Challenges and Opportunities for Growth.* Rep. Institute for Societal Leadership, Singapore Management University, n.d. Web. 12 June 2017. http://isl.smu.edu.sg/sites/default/files/isl_smu_edu_sg/CIL/Indonesia%20CIR%20%208Final%20Draft%29.pdf

204. Sakai, Minako. "Building a Partnership for Social Service Delivery in Indonesia: State and Faith-based Organisations." *Australian Journal of Social Issues*, 47.3 (2012): 373–88. *ProQuest*. Web. 12 June 2017.
205. Antlöv, Hans, Rustam Ibrahim, and Peter van Tuijl. *NGO Governance and Accountability in Indonesia: Challenges in a Newly Democratizing Country*. Publication. The International Center for Not-for-Profit Law. July 2005. Web. 12 June 2017. http://www.icnl.org/research/library/files/Indonesia/Peter_NGO%20accountability%20in%20Indonesia%20July%2005%20version.pdf
206. Sakai, Minako. "Building a Partnership for Social Service Delivery in Indonesia: State and Faith-based Organisations." *Australian Journal of Social Issues*, 47.3 (2012): 373–88. *ProQuest*. Web. 12 June 2017.
207. Ellington, John W. *The Indonesia Report: National Landscape, Current Challenges and Opportunities for Growth*. Rep. Institute for Societal Leadership, Singapore Management University, n.d. Web. 12 June 2017. http://isl.smu.edu.sg/sites/default/files/isl_smu_edu_sg/CIL/Indonesia%20CIR%20%208Final%20Draft%29.pdf
208. Latief, Hilman. Rev. of *Faith and the State: A History of Islamic Philanthropy in Indonesia. Brill's Southeast Asian Library, v. 1. By Amelia Fauzia. Pacific Affairs*, 88.1 (2015): 231–33. *ProQuest*. Web. 12 June 2017.
209. Kloos, David. "Review: Faith and the State. A History of Islamic Philanthropy in Indonesia by Amelia Fauzia." *Bijdragen Tot De Taal-Land- En Volkenkunde*, 170.4, Colonial Re-Collections: Memories, Objects, and Performances (2014): 576–79. *JSTOR*. Web. 12 June 2017. http://www.jstor.org/stable/10.2307/43817977?ref=search-gateway:271a139c5808db8c6a9014c0683e223b
210. Fauzia, Amelia. "Faith and the State: A History of Islamic Philanthropy in Indonesia." Thesis. The University of Melbourne. 2008. Web. 12 June 2017. http://minerva-access.unimelb.edu.au/bitstream/handle/11343/35228/118527_amelia%20thesis.pdf?sequence=1
211. Osili, Una, and Çağla Ökten. "Giving in Indonesia: A Culture of Philanthropy Rooted in Islamic Tradition." *The Palgrave Handbook of Global Philanthropy*. Ed. Femida Handy and Pamala Wiepking. Basingstoke: Palgrave Macmillan, 2015, 388–403. Print.
212. Fuad, Muhammad. "Civil Society in Indonesia: The Potential and Limits of Muhammadiyah." *Sojourn: Journal of Social Issues in Southeast Asia*, 17.2 (2002): 133–63. *JSTOR*. Web. 12 June 2017. http://www.jstor.org/stable/10.2307/41057084?ref=search-gateway:12190cda0c195f470c043af834c803f5
213. Ibrahim, Rustam. *CIVICUS Civil Society Index Report for the Republic of Indonesia*. Rep. Yappika, 2006. Web. 12 June 2017. http://www.civicus.org/media/CSI_Indonesia_Country_Report.pdf

214. Antlöv, Hans, Rustam Ibrahim, and Peter van Tuijl. *NGO Governance and Accountability in Indonesia: Challenges in a Newly Democratizing Country*. Publication. The International Center for Not-for-Profit Law. July 2005. Web. 12 June 2017. http://www.icnl.org/research/library/files/Indonesia/Peter_NGO%20accountability%20in%20Indonesia%20July%2005%20version.pdf
215. Kimura, Ehito. "State, Society, and Society: The Case of Indonesia." *Harvard Asia Pacific Review*, 7.1 (2003): 50–53. *ProQuest*. Web. 12 June 2017.
216. *Strengthening Philanthropy in the Asia Pacific: An Agenda for Action—Background Paper: Indonesia*. Rep. Asia Pacific Philanthropy Consortium. July 2001. Web. 12 June 2017. http://unpan1.un.org/intradoc/groups/public/documents/apcity/unpan005484.pdf
217. Sakai, Minako. "Building a Partnership for Social Service Delivery in Indonesia: State and Faith-based Organisations." *Australian Journal of Social Issues*, 47.3 (2012): 373–88. *ProQuest*. Web. 12 June 2017.
218. Antlöv, Hans, Rustam Ibrahim, and Peter van Tuijl. *NGO Governance and Accountability in Indonesia: Challenges in a Newly Democratizing Country*. Publication. The International Center for Not-for-Profit Law. July 2005. Web. 12 June 2017. http://www.icnl.org/research/library/files/Indonesia/Peter_NGO%20accountability%20in%20Indonesia%20July%2005%20version.pdf
219. Antlöv, Hans, Rustam Ibrahim, and Peter van Tuijl. *NGO Governance and Accountability in Indonesia: Challenges in a Newly Democratizing Country*. Publication. The International Center for Not-for-Profit Law. July 2005. Web. 12 June 2017. http://www.icnl.org/research/library/files/Indonesia/Peter_NGO%20accountability%20in%20Indonesia%20July%2005%20version.pdf
220. Antlöv, Hans, Rustam Ibrahim, and Peter van Tuijl. *NGO Governance and Accountability in Indonesia: Challenges in a Newly Democratizing Country*. Publication. The International Center for Not-for-Profit Law. July 2005. Web. 12 June 2017. http://www.icnl.org/research/library/files/Indonesia/Peter_NGO%20accountability%20in%20Indonesia%20July%2005%20version.pdf
221. Ellington, John W. *The Indonesia Report: National Landscape, Current Challenges and Opportunities for Growth*. Rep. Institute for Societal Leadership, Singapore Management University, n.d. Web. 12 June 2017. http://isl.smu.edu.sg/sites/default/files/isl_smu_edu_sg/CIL/Indonesia%20CIR%20%208Final%20Draft%29.pdf
222. Osili, Una, and Çağla Ökten. "Giving in Indonesia: A Culture of Philanthropy Rooted in Islamic Tradition." *The Palgrave Handbook of Global Philanthropy*. Eds. Femida Handy and Pamala Wiepking. Basingstoke: Palgrave Macmillan, 2015, 388–403. Print.

223. *Strengthening Philanthropy in the Asia Pacific: An Agenda for Action—Background Paper: Indonesia*. Rep. Asia Pacific Philanthropy Consortium, July 2001. Web. 12 June 2017. http://unpan1.un.org/intradoc/groups/public/documents/apcity/unpan005484.pdf
224. Ibrahim, Rustam. *CIVICUS Civil Society Index Report for the Republic of Indonesia*. Rep. Yappika, 2006. Web. 12 June 2017. http://www.civicus.org/media/CSI_Indonesia_Country_Report.pdf
225. Ellington, John W. *The Indonesia Report: National Landscape, Current Challenges and Opportunities for Growth*. Rep. Institute for Societal Leadership, Singapore Management University, n.d. Web. 12 June 2017. http://isl.smu.edu.sg/sites/default/files/isl_smu_edu_sg/CIL/Indonesia%20CIR%20%208Final%20Draft%29.pdf
226. Osili, Una, and Çağla Ökten. "Giving in Indonesia: A Culture of Philanthropy Rooted in Islamic Tradition." *The Palgrave Handbook of Global Philanthropy*. Eds. Femida Handy and Pamala Wiepking. Basingstoke: Palgrave Macmillan, 2015, 388–403. Print.
227. Osili, Una, and Çağla Ökten. "Giving in Indonesia: A Culture of Philanthropy Rooted in Islamic Tradition." *The Palgrave Handbook of Global Philanthropy*. Eds. Femida Handy and Pamala Wiepking. Basingstoke: Palgrave Macmillan, 2015, 388–403. Print.
228. *Strengthening Philanthropy in the Asia Pacific: An Agenda for Action—Background Paper: Indonesia*. Rep. Asia Pacific Philanthropy Consortium. July 2001. Web. 12 June 2017. http://unpan1.un.org/intradoc/groups/public/documents/apcity/unpan005484.pdf
229. Antlöv, Hans, Rustam Ibrahim, and Peter van Tuijl. *NGO Governance and Accountability in Indonesia: Challenges in a Newly Democratizing Country*. Publication. The International Center for Not-for-Profit Law. July 2005. Web. 12 June 2017. http://www.icnl.org/research/library/files/Indonesia/Peter_NGO%20accountability%20in%20Indonesia%20July%2005%20version.pdf
230. Hedman, Eva-Lotta E. "Contesting State and Civil Society: Southeast Asian Trajectories." *Modern Asian Studies*, 35.4 (2001): 921–51. *JSTOR*. Web. 10 July 2017. http://www.jstor.org/stable/10.2307/313196?ref=search-gateway:b64560a9575aeb19023ff5fb77cb6fcb
231. Cogswell, Elizabeth Agee. "Private Philanthropy in Multiethnic Malaysia." *Macalester International* 13th ser. 12.1 (2002): 105–21. Web. 10 July 2017. http://digitalcommons.macalester.edu/macintl/vol12/iss1/13
232. Hedman, Eva-Lotta E. "Contesting State and Civil Society: Southeast Asian Trajectories." *Modern Asian Studies*, 35.4 (2001): 921–51. *JSTOR*. Web. 10 July 2017. http://www.jstor.org/stable/10.2307/313196?ref=search-gateway:b64560a9575aeb19023ff5fb77cb6fcb

233. Hilton, Matthew. "The Consumer Movement and Civil Society in Malaysia." *International Review of Social History*, 52.3 (2007): 373–406. *ProQuest*. Web. 10 July 2017.
234. Hilton, Matthew. "The Consumer Movement and Civil Society in Malaysia." *International Review of Social History*, 52.3 (2007): 373–406. *ProQuest*. Web. 10 July 2017.
235. Hedman, Eva-Lotta E. "Contesting State and Civil Society: Southeast Asian Trajectories." *Modern Asian Studies*, 35.4 (2001): 921–51. *JSTOR*. Web. 10 July 2017. http://www.jstor.org/stable/10.2307/313196?ref=search-gateway:b64560a9575aeb19023ff5fb77cb6fcb
236. Hilton, Matthew. "The Consumer Movement and Civil Society in Malaysia." *International Review of Social History*, 52.3 (2007): 373–406. *ProQuest*. Web. 10 July 2017.
237. Hilton, Matthew. "The Consumer Movement and Civil Society in Malaysia." *International Review of Social History*, 52.3 (2007): 373–406. *ProQuest*. Web. 10 July 2017.
238. Hedman, Eva-Lotta E. "Contesting State and Civil Society: Southeast Asian Trajectories." *Modern Asian Studies*, 35.4 (2001): 921–51. *JSTOR*. Web. 10 July 2017. http://www.jstor.org/stable/10.2307/313196?ref=search-gateway:b64560a9575aeb19023ff5fb77cb6fcb
239. Cogswell, Elizabeth Agee. "Private Philanthropy in Multiethnic Malaysia." *Macalester International* 13th ser. 12.1 (2002): 105–21. Web. 10 July 2017. http://digitalcommons.macalester.edu/macintl/vol12/iss1/13
240. Hedman, Eva-Lotta E. "Contesting State and Civil Society: Southeast Asian Trajectories." *Modern Asian Studies*, 35.4 (2001): 921–51. *JSTOR*. Web. 10 July 2017. http://www.jstor.org/stable/10.2307/313196?ref=search-gateway:b64560a9575aeb19023ff5fb77cb6fcb
241. Cogswell, Elizabeth Agee. "Private Philanthropy in Multiethnic Malaysia." *Macalester International* 13th ser. 12.1 (2002): 105–21. Web. 10 July 2017. http://digitalcommons.macalester.edu/macintl/vol12/iss1/13
242. Cogswell, Elizabeth Agee. "Private Philanthropy in Multiethnic Malaysia." *Macalester International* 13th ser. 12.1 (2002): 105–21. Web. 10 July 2017. http://digitalcommons.macalester.edu/macintl/vol12/iss1/13
243. Cogswell, Elizabeth Agee. "Private Philanthropy in Multiethnic Malaysia." *Macalester International* 13th ser. 12.1 (2002): 105–21. Web. 10 July 2017. http://digitalcommons.macalester.edu/macintl/vol12/iss1/13
244. Cogswell, Elizabeth Agee. "Private Philanthropy in Multiethnic Malaysia." *Macalester International* 13th ser. 12.1 (2002): 105–21. Web. 10 July 2017. http://digitalcommons.macalester.edu/macintl/vol12/iss1/13
245. Weiss, Meredith L. "Edging Toward a New Politics in Malaysia: Civil Society at the Gate?" *Asian Survey*, 49.5 (2009): 741–58.

JSTOR. Web. 10 July 2017. http://www.jstor.org/stable/10.1525/as.2009.49.5.741?ref=search-gateway:c9610f1e926f25fc951babb76622aa30

246. Weiss, Meredith L. "Edging Toward a New Politics in Malaysia: Civil Society at the Gate?" *Asian Survey*, 49.5 (2009): 741–58. *JSTOR*. Web. 10 July 2017. http://www.jstor.org/stable/10.1525/as.2009.49.5.741?ref=search-gateway:c9610f1e926f25fc951babb76622aa30
247. Weiss, Meredith L. "Edging Toward a New Politics in Malaysia: Civil Society at the Gate?" *Asian Survey*, 49.5 (2009): 741–58. *JSTOR*. Web. 10 July 2017. http://www.jstor.org/stable/10.1525/as.2009.49.5.741?ref=search-gateway:c9610f1e926f25fc951babb76622aa30

CHAPTER 3

Changing Laws or Taxing Changes: Policies in Flux

Ruth A. Shapiro

Asia isn't the only place to experience a trust deficit. Trust has fallen to discouraging levels around the world, according to the 2017 "Trust Barometer" by Edelman, a public relations firm. Titling its recent report "An Implosion of Trust," Edelman writes that trust in NGOs in the United States, China, Japan, Germany, and the UK fell to less than 50 percent, its lowest level since 2001, when the survey was first conducted. In Asia, trust for civil society has been low for many years, and it has recently fallen further in Japan, South Korea, Singapore, and Malaysia.

But there are bright spots. Trust levels have actually increased in India, China, and Hong Kong, for reasons that may be duplicated elsewhere. These economies have taken steps to clarify the murky landscape in which private social investment takes place, a problem detailed in Chapter 4. China, especially, has received media attention over new laws affecting international NGOs. Though China and India are at the forefront of changing the environment for charitable action, other nations are also amending laws aimed at the giving and receiving of funds. Some changes reflect a desire on the part of governments to mitigate the trust deficit and allow for greater transparency and accountability. Some have to do with entirely different agendas.

Changes in the legal system affecting philanthropy broadly fall into three categories. The first is an effort by governments to discern between

R.A. Shapiro
CAPS, Hong Kong SAR, China

R.A. Shapiro et al., *Pragmatic Philanthropy*,
https://doi.org/10.1007/978-981-10-7119-5_3

advocacy and social delivery organizations, with the goal of permitting the latter while hindering the former, especially when such groups advocate for policies counter to the government's agenda. Within those regulations lies a subordinate set aimed at curtailing foreign funding oriented toward changes in individual rights, freedom of speech, and political engagement. The governments in question find this outside involvement an infringement of authority, and they have little or no interest in permitting foreign organizations to meddle with official aims. The second category includes policies aimed at increasing local philanthropy, particularly when it is in line with the government's agenda, and the third set is of laws endeavoring to create more transparency and accountability. On this last count, many governments are aware that if the trust deficit can be mitigated, increased local giving could result. This chapter examines the policies governing civil society in each of these three categories.

The definition of civil society is difficult to pin down. In fact, in 2001, the BBC stated, "The paradox about civil society is that it covers a vast range of activities—yet it's very hard to define." In an attempt to address this difficulty, the BBC produced a 12-part series called *What Is Civil Society?*[1] Despite this noble effort, the definition still evades us, although we can all agree that facets, goals, and operating norms of civil society differ across cultural contexts. The details give context to the current legal changes in Asia.

Civil society is often thought of as the voice and actions of the people, instead of that of companies and of the government. In the Western context, it is considered a basic tenet of a pluralistic society. While not necessarily the case, the term is often used as a contrarian voice against the government and the private sector. Civil society tends to focus on human rights and social justice. Civic engagement is a different story. Civic engagement is the way in which ordinary people can participate in helping their communities and countries, and the term does not carry an antagonistic connotation. Although civic engagement can utilize both political and non-political processes, it is not about pluralism as an endgame but of the human tendency to help one another. But the distinction can become complex. Many efforts start off as engagement only to become advocacy, and vice-versa. It often becomes clear to those trying to solve a problem that systemic change must include the government, and sometimes that implies the government must also change. Over the past decade, we can see a trend in Asia to channel energy into civic engagement while trying, at times with great conviction, to curtail the growth of civil society. As Simon Andrew Avenell writes when talking about the creation of the NPO (nonprofit organization) law in Japan, "Never did they [civil society pioneers] imagine that their model would become an endorsement of the state's mellifluous vision of civil society."[2]

A good portion of recent regulatory change aims at tamping down organizations that promote a political agenda contrary to the government's goals. Such regulations stem from the perception that many political agendas are funded by foreign actors; while it is difficult to determine precise figures, that might be partially true. Within Asian nations, donors might have little interest in challenging the system. In Chapter 4, we note that many Asian philanthropists have become wealthy under the status quo and therefore see no reward from agitating for social and political change (except in extreme cases such as the People Power revolution in the Philippines). In fact, the whole lobbying industry is almost absent in Asian nations as corporate leaders choose to either go along with the government or find ways to work around existing statutes. One cannot equate the government-friendly Keidanren in Japan or the Federation of Korean Industries in Korea with the Business Roundtable or the offices that line K Street in Washington D.C.

Asia is not unique in grappling with the intent of an organization and thus calibrating government support based on perceptions of the advocacy aims of an organization. The United States put tax policies in place in 1913 to delineate between organizations with strictly social missions and those that include in their mandate lobbying for policy change. Despite these laws being on the books for more than a century, there are frequent examples of organizations crossing the line between social delivery and advocacy. In recent years, with the rise of social enterprises, a new gray area between profit and nonprofit has emerged that challenges historical thinking and practice about organizations delivering social good.

And as in other parts of the world, Asia sees friction at the intersection between nonprofit and religious organizations. In most every country where there are tax-exemption policies, religious organizations enjoy these benefits. Normally, their work—such as help for the needy—passes without incident. Sometimes, however, the goals of the organization counter those of the government, as seen in Indonesia in July of 2017, when President Joko Widodo signed a decree making it easier to disband religious or civil society organizations. The decree was broadly seen as being aimed at Hizbut Tahrir, a conservative Islamic organization at odds with the national constitution and pluralist state ideology. Even as many understood why the Jokowi administration would seek to quash Hizbut Tahrir's efforts, human rights groups swiftly expressed concern that the law could be used to disband any politically inconvenient civil society groups, regardless of their religious persuasion. "This threatens the legal rights of all NGOs in Indonesia," said Usman Hamid, the Indonesia director of Amnesty International.[3]

Another religious organization, the Rashtriya Swayamsevak Sangh (RSS) has been disbanded three times in its history, while the Congress party ruled India. The RSS, considered to be the largest nonprofit in the world with an estimated 2.5 million members, is a Hindu nationalist organization with the motto of "Selfless Service to the Motherland." Now in favor with the Modi government, the RSS has expanded efforts to obstruct the work of nonprofits aligned with other religions.

The primary tool of hindering religious and political voices has been a crackdown on organizations receiving funding from abroad. In the past few years, the two Asian countries that have been most active in endeavoring to control foreign funding of NGOs are China and India. In 2010, India passed the Foreign Contributions Regulation Act (FCRA), prohibiting the use of overseas funds for "activities detrimental to the national interest." Though the law was initially seen as a bureaucratic burden, entailing significant financial reporting and documentation, the effects have recently become more severe. Under the Modi government, elected in 2014, FCRA requirements of filing annual returns have been used to cancel registrations of more than 10,000 organizations while denying renewals of an additional 1300 found to have filed incorrect information.[4] The reporting requirements imposed through FCRA are so onerous that many nonprofit organizations forego foreign contributions altogether.

Others closed their doors. The FCRA legislation shut down Colorado-based nonprofit Compassion International, which had been operating in India for 48 years to provide educational, health, and nutritional services for children. According to *The New York Times*, it has repeatedly ranked as India's largest single foreign donor, transferring around $45 million a year.[5] But FCRA regulations accused it of funding religious conversions, a charge it denies. FCRA rules were also instrumental in shuttering the India operations of the Open Society Foundation and of Greenpeace.

Among the most contentious moves has been the decision to cancel the license of PHFI (Public Health Foundation of India). PHFI has received a significant portion of its support from the Bill and Melinda Gates Foundation to provide its health-related services. Some commentators have said that the decision was based on PHFI's and the Gates Foundation's anti-smoking programs, while others have cited the relationship between the Gates Foundation, GAVI (the Vaccine Alliance), and various international pharmaceutical firms. The PHFI has filed an appeal, and as of now is waiting to hear from the government about reinstatement of its license.

China's new international NGO (INGO) law goes beyond funding. The goal of the law is to allow for greater management and control of foreign NGOs and foundations operating in China. The official language says, "This law is designed to standardize and guide all activities carried out by overseas NGOs within China, and protect their rights and interests, while promoting communication and cooperation."[6]

In practice, the new system creates the need for dual registration for overseas NGOs (this includes nonprofit organizations; think tanks; and social organizations, including associations). They need to satisfy two criteria for legal status in China. First, they must have an appropriate government department act as a professional supervising unit, and second, they must register with public security authorities. The new law requires the NGOs to find a sponsor before registering, making this key to forming a legal entity.

The burden is placed on the sponsor to decide if the international NGO is engaged in appropriate activities and to oversee their activities. This poses a formidable hurdle, especially for those organizations relatively new to China or engaged in any activity a local partner might consider risky. Foreign organizations approved to date have had long-standing relationships with local partners, with a somewhat even split of organizations involved with trade and the others focused on more humanitarian pursuits. In the first six months of the law, just 154 organizations had been approved: 71 were trade-elated, such as Cotton US and the France Chamber of Commerce, and many counted for several listings; World Vision, a humanitarian organization, was listed six times with approval from the provinces of Guangdong, Guangxi, Guizhou, Jiangxi, Tianjin, and Yunnan. The Ford Foundation and the Bill and Melinda Gates Foundation, both organizations facing challenges in India, were approved in China during the first round.[7]

There has been a great deal of international media attention regarding China's new INGO law. Finding a supervising unit might not be easy. There is very little upside, and potential significant downside, for the Chinese supervisor, though the burden may be eased when the work of a particular NGO aligns with the tasks of its governmental supervisory body. A further burden comes from the requirement that no INGO can be involved with political activities, a problem when the interpretation of what constitutes political activities can vary across time and disciplines.

For example, for many years, the number of Chinese with HIV/AIDS was listed as a state secret, making outreach in that area politically difficult. And if the NGO's work is multidisciplinary in nature, and does not fall clearly into a subject area (environment, health, education), it may be difficult to find a supervisory unit from a sector-specific ministry. Lastly, the role of the Ministry of Public Security is central to the new law but it is not clear how or which relevant MPS officials will be trained to deal with these new responsibilities. As in the case with many of China's laws, the specifics regarding implementation will be ironed out over time. In the meantime, with more than 7000 foreign NGOs in China, there are many NGO leaders who do not know if they will be able to continue with their work.

Increasing Local Philanthropy

This book is entitled *Pragmatic Philanthropy*. One of the clearest trends we witness across Asia is that of Asian donors providing philanthropic support in line with, and at times in partnership with, the government's agenda for addressing social challenges. This is a common trend. For many years, as wealth increased, a number of governments did not seem to grasp why private money might be helpful. They grappled with the notion that by allowing funding for education, health care, or disaster relief, there might be a perception that government itself wasn't doing its job by dealing with these issues directly. In a number of meetings I've had with government officials, they questioned why philanthropy was necessary when it was the government's role to provide education and health care. This was especially the case in China.

More recently, however, several governments in Asia, including China, have come to the realization that Asian philanthropists tend to want to support government initiatives and will make donations that are aligned with government goals. In our work, we see how this trend paves the way for governments to craft laws encouraging local giving.

Official support for the sector can be seen most clearly in the creation of tax subsidies for the giving and receiving of philanthropy. Here, Singapore is a dramatic outlier. In order to spur local giving, Singapore raised its tax subsidy to 250 percent in 2011, and in some cases provides matching funds. In 2015, the tax subsidy was increased to 300 percent until the end of 2018 to celebrate the island state's jubilee year. The Singapore *Straits Times* quoted Finance Minister Tharman Shanmugaratnam who said: "On the occasion of our jubilee year, we should take the opportunity to engage in giving to the causes that we feel matter to us as Singaporeans."[8]

The very context of giving must be seen through an Asian lens. In their book *Charitable Giving and Tax Policy*, Gabrielle Fack and Camille Landais look at the relationship between philanthropy and tax policies in the United States, the United Kingdom, Canada, and Denmark.[9] They use tax policies as a way to answer three questions: why do people give, what constitutes a public good, and does enforcement of tax policies affect people's behavior or is it enough to have the rules on the books? But these questions carry significant Western assumptions, as the authors note it is difficult to assign a monetary value to the "warm glow" generated by a philanthropic contribution. In Asia, while the altruistic aspect of providing a contribution does exist, so does the notion of the benefit of enhancing relationships with business partners and with government, motivations missing from the Fack and Landais calculation. The second question can be seen as tautological in the Asian context; a public good is what the government determines is a public good. This may be explicit, such as the verbiage and directions in China's new charity law, or it can be implicit. When Narendra Modi championed the need for more toilets in India, there was a flurry of philanthropists building toilets throughout the country. Now some people say that there are not only enough toilets but that many of them are being used as storage facilities, as there was little if any concurrent sanitation education about the use, behavior, and benefits associated with toilets. Lastly, while the question of enforcement is relevant in the Asian context, the signaling aspect of government policy is again very important. Governments use policies to signal what matters and what does not, or what is encouraged and what is discouraged. In countries with weak civil society and strong governments, private individuals and companies become adept at reading between the lines of the actual policy itself. Singapore provides another good example. Fiscal incentives can be helpful, but given Singapore's low tax rate, subsidies do as much by providing a powerful message that the government encourages its citizens to give to local causes. These tax breaks are only available when a tax-paying Singaporean gives to certified nonprofit organizations doing work in Singapore, in activities approved by the government. Such a policy would be unthinkable in America, but not in China or the Philippines.

Of the 15 economies in the Centre for Asian Philanthropy and Society's Doing Good Index survey, only Indonesia does not grant any tax benefit to individuals and all of them provide some sort of tax subsidies to corporations. In practice, fewer countries make full use of their policies, because a government can really only offer a tax break when it is effectively collecting taxes. As many countries in Asia struggle with tax collection, offering tax subsidies may sound good on paper but might not amount to much in real monetary value.

It is also true that although tax relief may literally be part of the law, it can be very difficult for either the donor or the tax-exempt organization to claim these benefits. The process by which one gets tax-exempt status in China is particularly onerous. The Harvard Kennedy School report states that as of 2015, only 157 organizations had been granted tax-exempt status.[10] In our Doing Good Index, the time and expense of registering as a tax-exempt organization is part of our calculation of what enables or hinders a philanthropic ecosystem.

There are other ways to incent local giving, allowing a government to endorse citizens providing private support for local and national challenges. One of the most popular recent innovations is a national giving day, week, or month. In 2015, the Japanese government approved a consortium endeavoring to increase local philanthropic giving through a "Giving December" program to "reflect on the importance and roles of donations, increase interest in donating, and create an opportunity for action."

In China, the new charity law includes establishment of an official "charity week" and day. Many Internet companies, especially, have played up Charity Day. During its second annual Charity Day event last September, Internet giant Tencent raised US$44 million as 6.8 million users donated to an assortment of charities.[11] South Korea hosts a Giving Big Festival, and Thailand promotes Volunteer Day. In 2017, Singapore, through its quasi-governmental partners the National Volunteer and Philanthropy Centre and the National Council of Social Service, has organized Singapore Cares, a multifaceted program designed to "support the goodwill of Singaporeans and guide them to better help those in need."

India is trying a variety of policy and regulatory initiatives to change the local philanthropic landscape. In the most progressive policy along these lines, India has made corporate social responsibility mandatory, becoming the first country in the world to require such spending. From 2015 on, companies with annual revenues of INR10 billion (about US$150 million) must give 2 percent after-tax or net profit to charity. The impact on the charitable sector is immense. Critics charge that, like the toilet imperative, the policy was put into practice without the programmatic and infrastructure programs necessary to deal with such a large influx of funds. While this is certainly true, there is also no doubt that the new law has elevated corporate social responsibility (CSR) beyond the periphery to the center of business decisions, placing it very much into the minds and activities of executives and directors. Two years into the new law, companies are still scrambling to gain expertise. The few with previous experience in CSR are in great demand. As with China's new charity law, it will take years to see the real impact of such a sweeping policy or to gauge how much it moves the needle in addressing massive social inequities and challenges.

With the Indian CSR legislation as an outlier and while putting in place tax subsidies and establishing giving days demonstrate a government's interest in promoting local giving, most probably the best way to increase philanthropy is by addressing the trust deficit. Regulations can help improve transparency and accountability in the sector. Regulatory change affecting both the supply and demand for philanthropy has been taking place in a number of Asian countries in recent years.

In our recent study, the Doing Good Index, we asked representatives from 15 Asian economies if there had been a front-page headline regarding a scandal involving a nonprofit organization in the last two years. Ten of them answered that there had been and several of the remainder said that while a scandal had not taken place in the last two years, fundraising is still affected by scandals that took place prior to this date.

When such scandals take place, the government reacts. As noted in other chapters, a pivotal moment in China's social sector was the Guo Meimei episode, when Ms. Guo, an employee of an organization affiliated with the Red Cross in China posted pictures of herself with two luxury cars. While the Chinese government had been formulating a charity law for some time, the policymaking process took on additional impetus during and after Ms. Guo's post and the public outrage and dismay that ensued.

The Chinese government's opinion about philanthropy and nonprofit organizations has changed dramatically since 2008, often referred to as the "first year of civil society in China." In 2008, responding to reports on social media, individuals and organizations flocked to Sichuan province to help with relief efforts after a massive earthquake. When they arrived, government officials did not know how to engage with them and treated both local and foreign NGOs with wariness and suspicion, turning most of them away. By the time of the Ya'an earthquake five years later, the government had changed its policy and its reactions significantly.

Government officials realized that private money could be channeled into causes and problems identified by the government. NGOs were welcomed to help as long as they registered with the local coordinating office.[12] According to Ze Tao of the China Foundation Center in Beijing, in the last five years 700 new foundations have been set up each year in China.[13] The new charity law in China is meant to accelerate this trend. A recent Harvard Kennedy School report notes, "The intention of the new legislation is to regulate better the sector and encourage more giving by the wealthy to sectors prioritized by the Chinese government, while restricting giving to non-priority issues."[14] The Chinese Community Party has realized that private money can help them achieve their goals and can also be channeled and controlled to a significant extent.

China's new law is designed to manage domestic Chinese philanthropic and charitable activities, making both more transparent and accountable. The law covers two major areas: governmental oversight and nonprofit support and management. It does not include changes to the tax code regarding subsidies and tax-exempt status, but it is expected that new tax regulations will soon be issued. The charity law also categorizes different types of organizations into charitable organizations, foundations, private non-enterprise units, and social groups. Government oversight has several provisions to increase transparency, including government approval for online fundraising platforms and requirements that financial records and audited reports must be placed on government-designated platforms. The law also stipulates that overhead expenses cannot exceed 10 percent for organizations and foundations and 13 percent for social groups. Included in the law are descriptions of what types of expenses can be included in overhead costs.

The charity law also promises to increase government procurement of services from nonprofit and SDOs. For the most part, government procurement is a useful and constructive process. Government contracts help SDOs by providing sustainable and reliable income streams. They are also important as they legitimize organizations and lend credibility to the sector. The Eden Social Welfare Foundation in Taiwan receives half of its total budget through government contracts to provide services and programs for the disabled. The critique of government procurement is that it can contribute to mission drift and the transition of an SDO from a mission-driven organization to merely being a government contractor. This is more likely to happen when the government does not understand or appreciate the specialty or expertise of an organization and asks it to do reports and projects that keep it busy and funded but not necessarily in the areas it was created to serve.

India has also been endeavoring to increase transparency and accountability. Given the significant amount of additional funding available due to the CSR legislation, increased accountability is a national imperative. The FCRA requirements discussed earlier have had the dual goals of increasing accountability as well as blocking foreign support for causes deemed questionable by the Modi government.

It is not uncommon when a government makes policy in reaction to a scandal or widespread belief of correcting a wrong that the reaction can verge on zealousness. This seemed to be the case when the Indian government announced the Lokpal Act amendment in July 2016. The original intent of the Lokpal Act in 2010–2011 had been to require public servants—that is, government officials—to declare their assets so as to make the accumulation of wealth, and thus of corrupt practices, more difficult. As the years went by and the various parliamentary committees got involved with the bill, an amendment was passed that defined a public servant as anyone sitting on a board of trustees or in the senior management of a nonprofit organization that received foreign contributions exceeding 10 lakh rupees (about US$15,000) or receives one crore rupees (about US$160,000) from an Indian government agency or department in a calendar year. The July 2016 amendment required trustees and senior staff to provide a listing of all assets under his or her name and all family members to the government by the end of August 2016, whereupon the government would release this information to the public. Not surprisingly, this announcement caused widespread alarm verging on panic. It meant that someone who was doing the right thing by sitting on a nonprofit board would be subjected to having all his or her assets and that of his/her family made public. And it was retroactive three years! One nonprofit research institution I know about was supposed to have new board elections in mid-August. All of the proposed candidates withdrew from consideration. After appeals to the government and to Prime Minister Modi himself, the deadline was extended to December 31, 2016, so that lawsuits could be filed. Numerous were. Fortunately, a decision was taken to delay the Lokpal Act indefinitely. While transparency and accountability are important, penalizing well-meaning board members would be quite unconstructive. It is very helpful to have trustees with company and private sector experience on a nonprofit board. These trustees can help with better financial forecasting, accounting, and strategic planning. There should be mechanisms that incent them to spend free time on SDO boards, not penalize them for doing so.

It can also happen that to hold off an overeager government or to compensate for governmental inertia, nonprofit organizations collaborate to create voluntary schemes. The latter situation was the case when a group of voluntary organizations proposed a giving day in Japan, which was then supported by the government and made official.

In the Philippines in 1998, the Department of Finance recommended that only donations to the government's disaster relief program be made tax deductible as only these contributions could be validated as to how the funds were spent. Six of the largest NGO and foundation umbrella organizations reacted with a proposal to create a self-regulatory mechanism that would ensure the transparency and accountability of organizations that met a strict set of criteria. The Philippine Council for NGO Certification (PCNC) was created and received authorization from the government to certify eligible organizations. The PCNC has by far the most stringent criteria and vetting process in Asia and perhaps in the world. By 2017, more than 1300 nonprofit organizations and foundations have been certified, and the PCNC has been heralded as a model not only of nonprofit-government collaboration but also of a concerted effort to create a clean and accountable charitable sector.

Conclusion

In 2017, major events shaped the discourse on the governance of civil society in Asia. In China and India new sets of rules are set to influence greatly the evolution of how these two nations develop. The two new laws in China, taken together, show that the Chinese government is endeavoring to increase local philanthropy and NGOs, while discouraging foreign involvement. While there are foreign organizations that have forged the appropriate connections within China who will not be too negatively affected, there is a climate of caution in place that is affecting all. India, as well, is looking inward when it comes to social investments.

In China, civil society is not the only recipient of this cultural ethnocentrism. In recent weeks, the availability of VPNs (virtual private networks), the primary way that one could access international websites, has been shut down. This is all part of Xi Xinping's pushback against all things "Western." In fact, when he came to power in 2013, a document known popularly as Document #9 was widely circulated among Communist Party cadres. The document called for the end of seven taboo topics: Western constitutional democracy, universal values, civil society, neoliberalism, the Western concept of press freedom, historical nihilism, and questioning whether China's system is truly socialist. Within this context, the rules regarding philanthropy and nonprofit organization could be viewed as a small sliver of a larger plan.

Whether that is true or not, the at times uneasy coexistence between the people, the government, and the private sector will continue to experience friction. The charitable sector is especially prone to such friction given the lack of clarity of mandate coupled with the often opaque and questionable motives of individuals and organizations operating within its parameters.

Again this year, two governments are struggling with scandals arising from questionable philanthropic contributions. Deposed Korean President Park Geun-hye is currently on trial for, among other things, soliciting donations to a friend's foundation in return for political favors. Shinzo Abe in Japan is reeling from donations he and others made to a veterinarian school. It would not be surprising that once these two situations are resolved, the governments in Japan and Korea call for new laws to govern the sector. As discussed at the beginning of the chapter, the Jokowi administration in Indonesia has done just that.

Asia is a continent of extremes. Home to the second, third, and fifth largest economies—China, Japan, and India—Southeast Asia, taken as a whole, is the world's sixth largest economy. There is incredible wealth in the region, the great preponderance of which has been created in the last 50 years or less. Asia is also a region with immense social challenges. India still struggles with a literacy rate hovering around 75 percent according to the World Bank. In 2017, the Sustainable Development Solutions Network lists only Japan and Korea in the top 50 countries whose aggregate scores show attainment or progress in meeting all of the Sustainable Development Goals.[15]

Beyond these indicators, new challenges arising from the unequal distribution of wealth in a globalized world are creating unrest and volatility throughout the world, and Asia is no exception. Hong Kong, with the highest Gini coefficient in the world, is grappling with discontent about the stronger domination of China and the lack of economic as well as democratic opportunity this is perceived to cause.

Technology has had a multifaceted influence. Millions of eyes see the excess of an unequal world and the fraudulent behavior of corrupt individuals. But technology can also hurt trust in charitable organizations overall; when a Guo Meimei posts damning photos, they go viral within hours, if not minutes.

Given the confluence of greater wealth, stubborn inequity, and the growth of technology, there is no doubt that governments will continue to try to manage social organizations and philanthropy. Officials will enact policies and regulations in line with their long-term goals and in response to short-term crises. Some will help and many will give rise to unforeseen circumstances that, in turn, will provoke further response by governments and by civil society at large.

Notes

1. BBC World Service. "What is Civil Society?" Broadcast on July 5, 2001. http://www.bbc.co.uk/worldservice/people/highlights/010705_civil.shtml. Accessed June 10, 2017.
2. Avenell, Simon Andrew. "Civil Society and the New Civic Movement in Contemporary Japan: Convergence, Collaboration and Transformation." *Journal of Japanese Studies*, Vol. 35, No. 2.
3. Emmot, Jon. "Indonesia Sets Stage for Crackdown on Hard-Line Islamist Groups." July 12, 2017 https://www.nytimes.com/2017/07/12/world/asia/indonesia-sets-stage-for-crack-down-on-hard-line-islamist-groups.html. Accessed July 12, 2017.
4. DNA Daily News. "NGOs Asked to Validate Bank Accounts for Foreign Contributions." June 7, 2017. http://www.dnaindia.com/india/report-ngos-asked-to-validate-bank-accounts-for-foreign-contributions-2464693. Accessed June 10, 2017.
5. Barry, Ellen and Suhasini Raj. "Major Christian Charity is Closing India Operations Amid Crackdown." *New York Times*, March 7, 2017. https://www.nytimes.com/2017/03/07/world/asia/compassion-international-christian-charity-closing-india.html. Accessed March 8, 2017.
6. China Development Brief. "English Translation of China's New Law on Overseas NGOs." May 3, 2016.
7. China Development Brief. "Comprehensive List of Overseas NGOs Registered in China." June 16, 2017.
8. Ng, Kelly. "Tax Deduction of 300% for Donations This Year." *Today*, February24,2015.http://www.todayonline.com/singapore/tax-deduction-300-donations-year. Accessed July 28, 2017.
9. Fack, Gabriel and Camille Landais (eds). *Charitable Giving and Tax Policy.* Studies of Policy Reform. Oxford University Press, Oxford, UK, 2016, pp. 18–19.

10. Johnson, Paula and Tony Saich. "Values and Vision: Perspectives on Philanthropy in 21st Century China". Harvard Kennedy School, Ash Center for Governance and Innovation Report, June 2017.
11. https://www.forbes.com/sites/russellflannery/2017/05/22/how-chinas-social-media-giant-tencent-is-shaking-up-traditional-philanthropy/#683ec12a7e6c. Accessed July 28, 2017.
12. Shapiro, Ruth A. 真正的问题解决者:社会企业如何用创新改变世界. "The Real Problem Solvers" Cheers Publishing, Beijing, China, 2014.
13. Macan-Markar, Marwaan. "Asia Gets Wise to the Art of Giving." *Nikkei Economic Review*, June 30, 2017.
14. Johnson, Paula and Tony Saich. "Values and Vision: Perspectives on Philanthropy in 21st Century China." Harvard Kennedy School, Ash Center for Governance and Innovation Report, June 2017.
15. Sustainable Development Solutions Network. "SDG Index and Dashboards Report2017."http://sdgindex.org/assets/files/2017/2017-SDG-Index-and-Dashboards-Report--regions.pdf. Accessed July 14, 2017.

CHAPTER 4

Philanthropists in Asia: What Do They Want? What Do They Get?

Ruth A. Shapiro

Asia's story of the past few years includes rising wealth and increased philanthropic giving. In 2014, there were 128 charitable contributions of more than US$1 million from Hong Kong alone, a 185 percent rise from the year before (and including the US$1.18 billion that Jack Ma of Alibaba used to set up his own foundation).[1] In its 2016 study on philanthropy, BNP Paribas says that 27 percent of high-net-worth Asians plan to leave at least a third of their fortune to charity.[2] With much greater wealth, many more Asians are becoming philanthropic, and the number and amounts of donations are increasing, in many cases, dramatically.

In responding to the increased interest, magazines, articles, and conferences on philanthropy and social investment have proliferated. In China alone, new magazines include *Charitarian*, *China Philanthropist*, and *Philanthropy*. *Forbes* magazine has been publishing a Heroes of Asian Philanthropy edition annually for the past nine years. These publications and related surveys offer a peek at the sources of donations as well as at the sectors receiving them. Overwhelmingly, education gets top billing as the focus of giving, followed by health. We wanted a further understanding of not only what Asian philanthropists fund but why and how they do it.

In the past few years, I have interviewed numerous ultra-high-net-worth individuals. Without exception, they expressed a willingness to

R.A. Shapiro
CAPS, Hong Kong SAR, China

R.A. Shapiro et al., *Pragmatic Philanthropy*,
https://doi.org/10.1007/978-981-10-7119-5_4

increase their philanthropy if they felt that they could trust the organization or individual receiving their largesse. As discussed in Chapter 3, Asian charity functions within a system dealing with a profound lack of trust.

Before examining strategies philanthropists have developed to mitigate the trust deficit, it helps to understand why it even exists. There are five primary reasons. The first has to do with the importance of an enabling regulatory environment. Government plays a crucial role in incentivizing civic engagement.

To align incentives, improve transparency, and encourage more charitable engagement, it is important to encourage regulations, tax incentives, and the general societal predisposition toward the giving and receiving of donations. Donors are very much influenced by the regulatory and tax policies that govern philanthropy in a country. There are two reasons for this, economic and political. On the economic front, governments can encourage donors to be more philanthropic by putting in place regulatory and tax incentives to give more. The recent corporate social responsibility legislation in India is an example of the government orchestrating giving in a very large way: its impact is enormous, as we'll discuss shortly in the section "Rely on Your Own Network."

On the political front, governments can signal to donors that individual and corporate philanthropy is not only allowed but also welcomed. Singapore's recent decision to increase the tax benefit of a philanthropic donation to 250 percent is a good example. In fact, through our case study work, we have shown the impact of confusing or murky regulations on diminishing philanthropists' desire to provide donations commensurate with their financial resources and potential. As covered earlier, governments across Asia have been trying to address this situation by putting into place new laws, regulations, and programs meant to stimulate local giving.

For social delivery organizations (SDOs), the ability to register as a charity, to be tax-exempt, to receive tax-deductible contributions, and to seek government contracts with projects aligned with their mission are critical factors in determining success.

Just as there are best practices in management, there are best practices when it comes to government policies. Which work best? What are the results as well as the unintended consequences? If the government wants to encourage charitable giving, what policies can it put in place that best insure that outcome? Which policies do not? This is policy research that must be undertaken to help address the reality that donors, practitioners, and in most cases the government itself is not clear about the types and ramifications of policy decisions shaping the charitable sector.

The second important factor in explaining the trust deficit is an extraordinary lack of transparency and disclosure by SDOs, often as a result of an inability to explain and measure results. Most SDOs have been started by and are run by people who are trying to do the right thing. At the same time, many of these individuals lack the skills necessary to keep proper accounting, management, and human resource systems to explain in a transparent manner how they spend the funds they raise and what impact their work is having. In a popular essay on philanthropy, Bill Gates explains, "You can achieve incredible progress if you set a clear goal and find a measure that will drive progress toward that goal," before he goes on to note, "it is amazing how often it is not done and how hard it is to get right."

Lack of metrics is not always the fault of SDOs. Government again plays a role: most Asian economies do not require financial transparency by SDOs, or their requirements are confusing. In the Philippines and South Korea, different ministries working in different sectors require different types of reporting from the organizations they are charged with overseeing. In some countries, no regular financial reporting at all is required. As noted earlier, in an attempt to remedy this shortfall, China enacted a new charity law in April of this year outlining financial reporting requirements and the government agencies tasked with oversight.

Foundations as well do not always have to be transparent, contributing to the trust deficit. Even venerable organizations such as the Tzu Chi Foundation in Taiwan are at risk of public condemnation when their finances are completely opaque. Some people believe that Taiwan's Tzu Chi Foundation is the wealthiest foundation in Asia, but it is a hard proposition to prove, or disprove. What is clear is that Tzu Chi, founded in 1966 by a highly respected nun, Chen Yen, is the world's largest Buddhist foundation. Tzu Chi, which means "compassionate relief," has enormous reach. With staff and volunteers totaling over 1 million people, operating in more than 40 countries, Tzu Chi has grown to be a formidable player in disaster relief and health services. It is also almost completely opaque, as Taiwan does not require religious organizations to provide accounting information. While it is known that Tzu Chi owns more than US$3 billion worth of Taiwanese real estate, there is no public record of how much the foundation is worth and how much it spends on charity. Most people agree that as long as the foundation runs under Chen Yen, now 79, it will stay true to its mission to promote "sincerity, integrity, trust, and honesty." Once she is gone, the test will be how it continues to operate in an environment without the need to be at all transparent.

Scandals are the third factor in explaining a widespread trust deficit. In systems where reporting and oversight is unclear, there can be significant and highly public scandals, most especially those that include fraud and the misuse of donated funds. In China, after the notorious incident of Guo Meimei, who had been caught apparently misspending donations to the Red Cross, philanthropic donations decreased by some estimates as much as 90 percent.[3] In the Philippines, the Pork Barrel Scandal was among the most notorious. This unsavory story involved the funding of "ghost projects" that were financed using funds provided to lawmakers for development projects. These projects were in turn "implemented" through fake foundations and non-governmental organizations set up by a firm with close ties to the government. Even in clean Singapore, there was an infamous scandal involving the widely respected Kidney Foundation, which was found to have committed fraud and provided its chief executive with lavish benefits not allowed by his contract. There are numerous other examples. In fact, in our The Doing Good Index study, in ten of the 15 economies studies reported front-page headline stories of scandals involving foundations and nonprofit organizations in the last two years.

The fourth powerful factor contributing to the trust deficit is confusion about the goals of the nonprofit organization itself. The term "NGO" itself makes no distinction between an advocacy organization and a social delivery organization. And many SDOs also advocate. Bainian Vocational Services in China advocates for increasing educational opportunities for migrant children. The World without Worries organization in South Korea advocates for an expanded view of what respectable tertiary education can look like. This type of advocacy is usually viewed by governments as benign or even constructive.

Problems occur when advocacy organizations agitate for changes in policy that are perceived to challenge the government's agenda. Groups that work on human rights, legal rights, and labor rights find that governments in Asia frown on their activities, or worse. We seek to make no judgment about the proper role of SDOs, but rather to explain what happens in context.

In more authoritarian regimes like China and Vietnam, Western advocacy organizations are simply not allowed to operate. In Korea, homegrown advocacy organizations stemmed from a citizen response to the years of dictatorship. In almost all cases, well-heeled Asian donors do not support organizations that are strictly focused on policy or regime change. Asian donors tend to focus on organizations that deliver a clear and unambiguous good to a needy population. Thus education and health care are the most popular causes supported by Asian donors: what government doesn't want a healthy, better-educated populace?

In the United States, such roles are more clearly defined. The tax code divides nonprofit organizations based on their goals and methodologies. Nonprofit organizations are 501(c)3s, the part of the tax code that enables both the organization to be tax exempt and the donor to receive a tax subsidy when making a contribution. 501(c)4s are civic organizations not organized for profit but with a mandate of pursuing a particular outcome often through lobbying or advocacy. Save the Children, the Red Cross, and the World Wildlife Fund are examples of American 501(c)3 organizations. Amnesty International, the Democratic National Committee, and Human Rights Watch are 501(c)4s. The system is not perfect, but it does help clarify distinctions.

No Asian country has this kind of legal separation, and the term NGO is often used across the spectrum. It is not a particularly useful term. Technically, NGO stands for "non-governmental organization," a problematic term that does not clarify the organization's goals to the donor or to the public at large. Even more confusing, many NGOs are, in fact, linked to government. A common acronym in the social sector in Asia is a GONGO, which is a government operated non-governmental organization—a term that for many seems contradictory to Western ears but makes sense within the Asian context. In South Korea, NGO is more used for an advocacy organization and the term NPO (for nonprofit organization) is used when referring to SDOs. This is also problematic, as many NPOs are utilizing social enterprises or business to augment their income. They are not, strictly speaking, nonprofits. In Japan, NGO refers to organizations focusing on helping developing countries and NPO is used when referring to domestic organizations.

We at the Centre for Asian Philanthropy and Society use the term *SDO*, or social delivery organization, to refer to an organization aiming to deliver a social good. SDOs may or may not have governmental connections, and they may be using business tools or social enterprises to achieve their goals, but they are distinct from pure advocacy organizations aiming to change public policy. That sort of designation can be particularly helpful in Asia, where donors rarely wish to cross officials at odds with challenging advocacy.

The last factor that leads to a trust deficit is the historic tendency of the "best and the brightest" to go into wealth-making or government careers instead of into the charitable sector. While there are many exceptions to this, many of the most highly educated people in Asia have chosen more lucrative career paths. In the past—in a poorer Asia—these choices made a great deal of sense. Now that many in the region are well off, or comfortably in the middle class, there are more opportunities for young people to take another route and spend time or their whole careers in the social sector. In 2016, Teach for the Philippines was listed by a Swedish firm as one of the top ten sought-after employers, an unlikely result even ten years ago. Young adults have also been excited by the advent of social enterprises, companies that run as a business but address a social need. Social enterprises are arising all over the region. In Hong Kong, Synergy Venture Network has helped to start 20 portfolio social enterprises since 2007. In South Korea, the Law on the Promotion of Social Enterprises was enacted in 2007, certifying 36 social enterprises. The numbers have been growing since.[4] Increased societal wealth and innovative business models bring new excitement into the social investment space. We expect to see more and more of the best and brightest choosing alternative careers in doing good.

Asia's trust deficit is not a static condition. While each of the above factors has contributed to the problem, many are improving. Policymakers, donors, the public, and those engaged in delivering social good all recognize that the need to fill this gap, to create mechanisms that engender trust. And in the meantime, philanthropists have developed a number of strategies designed to mitigate the existing trust deficit and the lack of institutional mechanisms for conducting due diligence.

But before talking about strategies, it is important to lay out motivation. What motivates someone with wealth to give it away in Asia? As shown in Chapter 2, there are long histories throughout the region showcasing benevolence on the part of those empowered through position or wealth, or both. The motivations for giving in Asia are consistent with giving in other parts of the world.

The most important motivation is compassion and a sense of humanity. Despite the jokes that wealthy people do not have hearts, those with wealth do care about the world and are part of it. In Asia, as in other places, people are motivated to give in order to help, in order to ease suffering, in order to find a cure, to educate a child, to help a mother. There are numerous examples of philanthropy in Asia going to the most basic human needs. Education, health care, and nutrition are at the top of those areas receiving support. This is especially true when there are natural disasters. Following the numerous extreme typhoons in the Philippines in recent years, flooding in Bangkok, and earthquakes in Japan and China, and the tragic 2004 tsunami, people have demonstrated extraordinary humanity and willingness to provide assistance.

Compassion also plays a role when determining the types of issues to support. David Wei of Shanghai built hospitals for Tibetan medicine in Tibet and Shanghai after witnessing the poor health-care infrastructure in Tibet. Laurel and George Tahija established a foundation focused on cultivating all children's learning potential in Indonesia, after finding these resources lacking when raising their own children.

There is also a strong paternalistic urge among Asians who have amassed wealth. It is not uncommon to hear those with wealth "helping the people" or "providing for the poor." There is a cultural affinity with taking care of those less fortunate in very much a paternalistic manner. Those receiving this assistance also buy into the notion of being taken care of. In his book *Blood and Silk*, writer Michael Vatikiotis quotes Malaysian Prime Minister Mahathir's daughter Marina Mahathir: "We are accustomed to tolerating the extraordinary wealth of our leaders. That is because we consider they deserve riches in return for looking out for us."[5] While this quote is referring to political leaders, it is also very much the case when it comes to business leaders. Communities expect those with wealth to provide for them. Those with wealth historically and still much in practice today feel it is their role to be the patriarch and take care of their extended family, relatives or not.

The cultivation and strengthening of relationships is another reason to give. People give when a friend or business associate asks for support of a cause or an organization that they have also been supporting. We will discuss this motivation in detail in the next section.

For many in business, a business imperative is reason to give. Many seek training and increased educational opportunities to raise the quality of employees. Others augment existing educational systems with their own training programs and courses.

And lastly, there is face, always a motivation in Asia. A philanthropist chooses to give so as to receive recognition for largesse. Of course, discerning cause and effect is a chicken-and-egg phenomenon. Does one give in order to get recognition or is recognition the reasonable and justifiable response to a generous act?

In any case, the social imperative for giving is growing in Asia. While some wealthy people resist the trend, most acknowledge the trend itself, one that affects not only the wealthy but also the middle class. Later on in this book, we will talk about the rise of crowdfunding throughout the region and its support among those with average incomes. Here we will address several key strategies employed by well-off philanthropists.

The most important strategy rests on the importance of relationships. Throughout history, Asia has been a region that has relied on relationships to conduct a host of activities. Businesses ranging from the *keiretsu* system in Japan to those shaped by Chinese clans have relied on relationships. Relationships created the social glue and incentives to carry out complex transactions in areas where rule of law has not been the dominant organizational principle.

It is not surprising that Nobel Laureate Muhammad Yunus based his microfinance model on the primacy of maintaining community and peer relationships. In Yunus' innovative structure, originally established in Bangladesh and now widely replicated, collateral was replaced by peer groups where all the members would be accountable if one did not repay a loan. It is only in recent years with the advent of international finance that mechanisms such as securities and exchange commissions, stock exchanges, and international accounting standards have been created to allow participation in global markets.

Despite these mechanisms, interactions based on relationships rather than transactions remain supremely important. This is not to say that relationships do not matter outside of Asia. Of course, they do, but in Asia, it is hard to overstate how much they do matter. Relationships often trump price, subject matter expertise and even at times, one's own interests. Much has been written about the importance of relationships in the private sector, and how-to books geared to novice Western businesspeople emphasize nurturing the relationships necessary for success in Asia.

In an area without a clear bottom line like philanthropy and social investment, the importance of relationships becomes even more decisive. Through our work, we have identified patterns of how relationships inform or even determine philanthropic decision-making.

Rely on Your Own Network

The most prevalent strategy employed by philanthropists in Asia is to rely on their own networks or sets of relationships. This happens in several ways.

The most common is that someone in your network asks you to donate to a cause that he or she is championing. Of course, this also happens in other parts of the world, as a dedicated board member or donor recruits friends and colleagues to support a particular organization. While the donation may be in fact going to a good cause, the primary reason behind the gift is to enhance the relationship of the donor with his or her friend or colleague. In fact, it is clear that the return on investment is calculated as the enhancement of the relationship first and perhaps the impact of the donation further down the list.

It is not uncommon to find a philanthropist whose total giving is reactive, based on friends' requests. While this is changing, there are still few philanthropists in Asia who decide on an issue or project first and then find the people and organizations to impact on that issue. In fact, as we will see, the great majority of philanthropic giving in Asia is reactive as compared with proactive, with the goal of ameliorating a particular problem.

An example of this was a donor who was asked by a friend to support an organization working with slum children. In an interview, he said, "I was not planning on donating to this cause, but of course it is a good one. Who doesn't care about slum children?" Then he quickly added, "Also, the person requesting was a business partner, so it was helpful all the way around."

Many donors employ this "I'll scratch your back if you scratch mine" strategy when it comes to philanthropy. Given the situation it is an elegant solution. The donor's risk is mitigated by the previous history of his friend or colleague with a particular organization; by giving, the relationship with that person deepens.

This response-approach also occurs regularly at the behest of a government official. In our work, we see two types of government requests to charitable causes. The first is when the government has a particular program or initiative for which they are looking to outsource much of the costs. This was what happened with our case study on the Squash Raquets Association of Malaysia (SRAM) in Malaysia. When the Malaysian government wanted to build up a national competency in the game of squash, it asked a prominent business leader to underwrite the associated costs. He obliged for several years and then passed the funding baton to another business leader who followed the same pattern. Another example is now taking place in India, where the government is not asking a company or donor to fund a specific project but has put in place incentives that amount to the same outcome. Since 2013, India has had an extraordinarily progressive CSR law requiring companies to spend 2 percent of after-tax profits for charitable causes. As we discussed in Chapter 3, it has generated a huge influx of cash going into social programs and projects. At the same time, Narendra Modi has been advocating for increased sanitation throughout the country. As a result, many businesses are building toilets. It is smart to do so: you are working toward meeting your 2 percent obligation while supporting Mr. Modi's agenda.

It is quite common in Asia for the government to ask local business leaders to pay for flagship projects that have societal value. In Korea, the large *chaebols* have all been asked to dedicate significant sums to pay for costs associated with the upcoming Olympic games. Once again, this is not idiosyncratic to Asia, but in Asia it is quite unthinkable for a company to say no.

Once again, it is not necessary for the government to ask overtly. On the homepage of the China Youth Development Foundation, a quasi-governmental organization dedicated to helping children in China, a banner headline reads, "Since 1989, donors like you have given ¥4.52 billion to our programs." You can then click on the list of donors, which includes many of the nation's top companies as well as a number of multinational companies. Giving to the China Youth Foundation is one degree removed from giving directly to the Chinese government.

In the examples above, the donor sees the triple benefits of providing support for a worthwhile cause while at the same time deepening relationships and mitigating the risks of making a donation into an unverified organization. In the case of the government, it may be in the donor's interest to show through philanthropy support for the government's goals.

There are costs to this approach, despite its efficiency in aligning incentives for donors. Sometimes, gifts from donors to the government for charitable work may not appear as noble. Given the existing lack of trust, the public can easily suspect foul play when the disbursement of funds is not transparent. An example of this can be seen in South Korea: in order to escape jail terms, both Hyundai's Chairman in 2006 and Samsung's chairman in 2008 donated $1 billion for charity to the government. In both cases, no records exist as to how the funds were disbursed, so it is easy to see why the public would be skeptical about their just use.

Philanthropists also use networks to direct donations through a person they trust. This happens in two ways. In the first case, the donor trusts a particular person and asks that person to head up an organization or an initiative that he supports. This was the case when Ronnie Chan, the chairman of the Asia Society, asked his long-term protégé to head the Asia Society's Hong Kong operations; he knew she could do an excellent job while also representing his interests. It was the case when Washington SyCip in the Philippines gave a large contribution to CARD, a microfinance organization, to put in a place a scholarship program. CARD was not an educational organization, but Wash SyCip trusted CARD's founder and CEO Aris Alip to figure out how best to take on this new task. In fact, it is not uncommon in Asia to ask someone you trust to take on a role or carry out a task regardless of whether that person has had similar experiences. In the United States, it is more common to look for a candidate who has had a relevant track record and then get to trust him or her. In Asia, it is often the other way around. In the end, the outcome is similar but the order of the steps toward that outcome differs in important ways.

The other way trust in a particular person matters is when that person is heading up an effort and relies on his or her network to gather support. This has certainly been the case for me personally, with support for the Centre for Asian Philanthropy and Society (CAPS). I have gone to those with whom I have had long and trusting relationships when asking for support. As Ronnie Chan said in a recent meeting, "I invest in people who I know will accomplish great things," and as Ratan Tata informed me, "I focus on those I trust."

Beginning with a trusted contact makes particular sense in Asia. Since there are few mechanisms for conducting due diligence on a social investment, the norm in Asia is to seek your friends' advice as to which organization does good work, which can be trusted. This means that within one economy, oftentimes the same organizations receive the bulk of the local community's support. The utility of relationships goes both ways. Donors use their relationships to decide who and what to give to; SDOs use theirs to solicit funds.

One of the ramifications of relying on one's network is the rise of what we are calling "superstar NGOs." In each economy there are a few nonprofit organizations that become well known and established among the elite. Giving to them becomes to a certain degree *de rigueur*. These organizations are headed by men and women who have either come from elite backgrounds themselves or have established themselves among the elite and gained their trust. Funding a superstar NGO is less risky. These organizations are well established and have a place of pride in the community. They have recognized names and lauded reputations. They often do excellent work. The downside is that by focusing one's giving on the most prominent organizations, the barrier to entry rises for new and potentially innovative organizations. It is very difficult to establish a new organization without a pre-existing set of enabling relationships. This difficulty is exacerbated by the existence of a small group of blue-chip organizations receiving the bulk of the philanthropic donations. In fact, in our study, in two of the economies, the Philippines and Malaysia, donors only wanted to fund case studies if it was with one particular organization. We convinced them to look beyond the one superstar NGO, but the initial desire to go with the most successful and best known was strong.

Philanthropists use their relationships in a variety of ways when making decisions about donations. Relationships may be the source of the request, the means by which to vet a request, or ultimately, the beneficiary of a request—even when a given contact falls outside of the issue or problem that is ostensibly the reason for the gift.

Faith-based Funding

Asian donors also give to faith-based organizations. As with others around the world, much of this giving is driven by the belief that these organizations embody the values of compassion, kindness, and doing good for one's fellow man. Faith-based giving often goes to SDOs that have been established by the clergy or lay practitioners closely associated with religious organizations. In our study, Haven of Hope in Hong Kong strives to maintain its Christian values while delivering secular health-care services. Caritas Manila benefits greatly as the charitable arm of the Catholic Church in a country where 86 percent of the population is Roman Catholic. Donors feel that their funds are being more effectively spent by organizations affiliated with their own religion.

Do It on Your Own

Since many philanthropists do not trust existing nonprofit organizations and are more confident of their own management and strategic abilities, some decide to fund their own foundations or SDOs. Most have financial skills and are active in their respective fields: Asia has very little inherited wealth that goes back more than a couple of generations. That means most high-net-worth individuals are businessmen and women who are engaged with their operations on a day-to-day basis. Increasingly, this means that many of them want to employ the same business rigor and savvy to their philanthropic investments as they do for their profit-making activities.

In Asia, companies are still family owned or dominated, to a large degree. The company's charitable contributions and those of its largest shareholder or owner are often indistinguishable. Zhang Xin and Pan Shiyi, for example, are the primary owners of SOHO China, and since they support educational initiatives, so does SOHO. Currently they focus on the provision of scholarships for promising Chinese students matriculated into several elite American universities. From 2008–2012, SOHO went directly into schools with its Children's Virtue Project and Bathroom Construction Campaigns. These two programs allow SOHO team members with relevant expertise and skills to work directly with schools.[6]

In India, Mukesh Ambani is the dominant shareholder of Reliance, with 45 percent of its shares, and his wife, Nita Ambani, chairs the Reliance Foundation. The Reliance Foundation works in five areas throughout India: rural transformation, education, health, urban renewal, and in arts, culture, and heritage. The Reliance Foundation follows the model of a philanthropist with faith in his or her own management skills: it is an operating foundation, meaning that it designs and carries out the projects itself, rather than giving the funds to existing SDOs.

Globally, foundations taking active roles in how their funds are spent are on the rise. In Hong Kong, the Jockey Club Charities Trust, the largest foundation in Hong Kong, has revamped its giving into strategic initiatives rather than supporting numerous and non-aligned organizations. The Azim Premji Foundation in India utilizes business strategies in addressing educational shortfalls in eight Indian states. It is extremely dynamic, forming one of the most strategic and ambitious foundations in the world and certainly in Asia.

Fund Foreign and Reputable Organizations

Our own chairman, Ronnie Chan, made international headlines when he and his brother Gerald made a contribution to Harvard University that was, at the time, the largest in its history. The T.H. Chan School of Public Health has now a large endowment to carry out cutting-edge research on global health pandemics.

The Chans are not alone. More and more Asians are donating abroad, in accordance with the principles outlined above, of supporting valuable causes and relying on existing contacts. Universities make natural recipients. According to *The Wall Street Journal*, Hong Kong donations make up 17 percent of the world's total donations to U.S. universities. Prior to the Chans' gift to Harvard, Princeton University ranked first among recipients, with US$67.6 million from Hong Kong donations, followed by Stanford University (US$39.3 million) and the University of California at

Berkeley (US$28.8 million).[7] In 2014, SOHO China's Pan Shiyi and Zhang Xin gave US$15 million to Harvard and US$10 million to Yale. In 2010, Chinese financier Zhang Lei gave US$8,888,888 to his alma mater, Yale University (8 being a lucky number in China). In 2010, Harvard Business School received US$50 million from Tata Companies, the Sir Dorabji Tata Trust, and the Tata Education and Development Trust.[8]

Nor do all the donations go to the United States. In May 2013, Li Ka-Shing of Hong Kong pledged £20 million (US$26.4 million) to Oxford University.[9] Dickson Poon of Hong Kong gave £10 million (US$13.2 million) the following year.[10]

Though these contributions caused some degree of backlash in their home economies, it is not unusual to donate to universities, especially an alma mater. Most of these donors gave large sums to universities in their home countries as well.

Conclusion

Philanthropy in Asia, like many other fields, is experiencing a cultural shift. With increased wealth, there is increased giving, resulting in many others moving up the learning curve of how and why to give.

For the man or woman on the street, the primary reason to give is the human tendency to be compassionate. For Lifeline Express, half of their donations in China and in Hong Kong come from small donations made without any type of quid pro quo. In Chapter 2, we saw how charity has a long and noble history in Asia. There continue to be many millions of donations made because the situation warrants it and people feel the very human desire to help. There is a reason that education is the largest beneficiary of philanthropic donations in Asia. Donors believe that education makes the most critical difference. All of the donors to our Centre have supported scholarships to one extent or another because of this heartfelt belief.

In addition, particularly for those making larger contributions, relationships continue to be a strong driver of charitable giving. Relying on relationships offers many advantages for donors. It is in fact a virtuous circle—you give, you enhance your relationships, which help you earn more, and thus you give more. In some ways, it is the most strategic thinking.

On the other hand, the desire to have impact, to make a difference, to solve a big problem, is also driving much philanthropic giving. Those who give to Western universities would argue that they are doing so to maximize the value. In the last few years, training programs and university courses on philanthropy have become to proliferate. Just a few months ago, the China Philanthropy Research Institute received US$50 million from five donors to establish the Shenzhen International Philanthropy Academy to train newly minted philanthropists on how best to give away their money. They draw from an active, growing pool in China.

Philanthropy, individual and corporate, is proliferating in Asia. As this book points out, it will maintain different characteristics from giving in the West but there is no doubt that it will continue to grow.

Notes

1. Coutts. 2015 Million Dollar Donors Report. http://philanthropy.coutts.com/en/reports/2015/executive-summary.html#wO0cSgP4b3ReE9Ao.99. Accessed May 11, 2016.
2. BNP Paribas. "New Philanthropy: Building Lasting Change." Executive Summary, 2016.
3. In 2011, Guo Meimei, 20, who claimed to hold a senior position at the Red Cross Society of China, posted evidence of lavish living on Weibo.
4. Korea Social Enterprise Promotion Agency "Korea Creates a Sustainable Ecosystem for Social Enterprises." http://www.socialenterprise.or.kr/eng/intro/greeting.do. Accessed June 19, 2016.
5. Vatiokis, Michael. *Blood and Silk*. Weidenfeld and Nicolson. London, UK. 2017, p. 91.
6. SOHO Foundation "Milestones." In SOHO Foundation Annual Report. SOHO China Official Corporate Site. http://www.sohochinafoundation.org/en/milestones. Accessed June 12, 2016.
7. Chow, Jason. "Hong Kong Tops List of Foreign Donors to US Schools." *Wall Street Journal*, September 22, 2014. http://www.wsj.com/articles/hong-kong-tops-list-of-donors-to-u-s-schools-1411401637. Accessed May 11, 2016.
8. Harvard Business School Press Release. "Harvard Business School Receives $50 million Gift from Tata Trust and Companies." October 14, 2010. http://www.hbs.edu/news/releases/Pages/tatagift.aspx. Accessed May 11, 2016.
9. University of Oxford News and Events. "Fundraising Campaign Reaches £2 billion and Counting." May 12, 2015. http://www.ox.ac.uk/news/2015-05-12-fundraising-campaign-reaches-%C2%A32-billion-and-counting. Accessed May 11, 2016.
10. University of Oxford China Centre Press Release. "Dickson Poon University of Oxford China Centre Building Opened." September 8, 2014. http://www.oxforduchina.org/the-oxford-china-centre.html. Accessed May 12, 2016.

CHAPTER 5

Who Do You Know SDO? Relationships Matter

Manisha Mirchandani and Ruth A. Shapiro

Relationships are two-way streets, connections between people, and donors know it—especially in Asia. As discussed in the chapter on philanthropists, donors use their relationships to engender trust and to guide decisions about funding. It's no surprise that our studies show successful social delivery organizations (SDOs) in Asia are adept at cultivating their own sets of relationships. Here we detail their strategies of employing relationships to get things done.

The most straightforward way to engage a helpful network is to have one in place from the start. Many successful SDOs begin with a founder or board member already established as a leader. Our board members are excellent examples. Ronnie Chan has been involved with numerous non-profit organizations for years, has led the Asia Society, and helped me to create first the Asia Business Council and now the Centre for Asian Philanthropy and Society. Lizzie Zobel is the co-founder of Sa Aklat Sisikat Foundation, a philanthropy devoted to increasing literacy, is the chairwoman of Teach for the Philippines, and sits on the board of the Population Council. Daniel Tsai sits on the board of his alma mater, the University of Southern California, and oversees four charitable foundations in Taiwan.

M. Mirchandani
CAPS, Hong Kong SAR, China

R.A. Shapiro
CAPS, Hong Kong SAR, China

R.A. Shapiro et al., *Pragmatic Philanthropy*,
https://doi.org/10.1007/978-981-10-7119-5_5

Jamshyd Godrej has been on the boards of the World Resources Institute, the World Wildlife Fund of India, Shakti Sustainable Energy Foundation, the Council on Energy, Environment and Water, and the National Center for Performing Arts. This group of leaders has made exceptional contributions to the charitable sector. Clearly when a person like Lizzie Zobel creates a new nonprofit organization, she not only legitimizes the effort but offers to it potential resources in ways that those without her network cannot.

In Asia, the involvement of the elite directly starting, running, and governing social delivery organizations is increasing with the rise in wealth. This "do it yourself" mentality—a spirit of philanthropic entrepreneurialism—is evident in many thriving SDOs. Elites have stepped in where government or existing social institutions have left a social need unfilled. One example is Nellie Fong, a legislator and chartered accountant, who caught the attention of Chinese authorities with her expertise on international tax law in the 1990s. She joined the transition team for the handover of Hong Kong from British to Chinese sovereignty and became aware of plans by China's provinces to send symbolic gifts for the occasion. Seeing an opportunity to respond in kind, she suggested a gift from the people of Hong Kong: a train that which could criss-cross mainland China, offering mobile health care to those who needed it. This idea was rooted in the very concept of *guanxi*, as a way for the people of Hong Kong to reciprocate the gifts received from the Mainland, and as a way of fostering goodwill.

With blessings from Hong Kong and Mainland officials, the Lifeline Express departed from Hong Kong on July 1, 1997, carrying eye doctors and equipment to perform cataract surgery in rural areas of China. Serving 130,000 beneficiaries and reaching 27 provinces and 120 cities since then, Lifeline Express was made possible through the tenacity of an insider like Fong. Her clout on both sides of the border helped her to garner support for the Eye Train concept, earning approval from two state-level ministries alongside multiple provincial and local officials in China—a prerequisite for nonprofits to operate openly and effectively in the country. Fong recognized her unique role as a convener to the extent that she personally drew up banquet seating arrangements when she brought people together in support of the cause. She used her personal *guanxi* to get the Eye Trains up-and-running and offered Lifeline Express as an opportunity for people to accrue it themselves: a seat on the board of the Lifeline Foundation would become an attractive platform for China's most influential current and former officials.

In Singapore, the Lien Foundation began with another well-established leader. Banker and entrepreneur Lien Ying Chow started the foundation in 1980 as a means of giving back to society. When it added professional staff in 2005–2006, its first hire was a former official and businessman, Lee Poh Wah. Brought on to lead Lien AID, an organization made "to champion the foundation's interests in water and sanitation," Lee encouraged its growth at a time when there was a paucity of SDOs focused on water-specific interventions.

Lien AID's substantial support from the Lien Foundation (about US$12 million by 2014, 80 percent of its operating income) enabled it to experiment with new solutions for improving the quality and availability of drinking water in the nearby countries of China, Vietnam, and Cambodia. With its financial security, Lien AID could experiment until discovering solutions that flourished in the local context. The organization's first project in Cambodia, in 2007, was as Lee put it, "our most spectacular failure." The hygiene complex constructed in an urban slum in the capital city of Phnom Penh became a target for resentment in the community and was eventually dismantled in 2012 to make way for property development in the fast-growing city. But Lien AID persisted in Cambodia with various water-related interventions, launching 43 successful community-based water social enterprises by May 2015. Today, Lee Poh Wah heads up the Lien Foundation as chief executive officer while Laurence Lien, grandson of Dr. Lien, serves as chairman of the board. Water and sanitation remains among its three areas of focus, and the foundation continues to be Lien AID's most generous benefactor, providing 91 percent of its income in 2013–2014. Responding to a gap in the social delivery sector, Lien AID was established as a "start-up," to bring about fresh ideas and to challenge existing norms. This was possible only with patient capital from its parent foundation, itself started by a leader in the community who could afford the risks associated with innovation.

Many donors move one step away from creating organizations themselves, looking to those who are already trusted members of their network. When Wash SyCip, Filipino business tycoon and founder of the Asian Institute of Management, got behind a project, there was one critical factor that drove his decision to do so: "I only fund organizations where I know and trust the leader," he said. He is not alone. Asian business has traditionally been conducted on the basis of good relations, as exemplified by the concept of *guanxi* in China. Translating roughly into English as "relationships," the phenomenon of Chinese business underpinned by personalized networks of influence has been closely studied in modern management literature. In the Oxford Handbook of Asian Business Systems, INSEAD Professor Michael Witt argues that business groups based on relationships exist due to the lack of rule of law and its formalized enforcement mechanisms.[1] There is great mistrust, which propels business people to stick with those they know.

Founders thus often establish a board of trustees where the relationships among them help move the organization forward. Of course, this is also true in successful organizations around the world, but given the cultural traditions and historical context of the region, it is particularly important in Asia. Bainian Vocational School (BNVS), for instance, chooses its board of trustees strategically to meet its mission in job placement. BNVS board members are well positioned both to help financially and to provide access to future company employers.

The China Medical Foundation (CMF) takes an additional step in targeting successful business leaders for its board. Unlike many other organizations, it requires a financial commitment of at least US$10,000 per annum from each board member. Many nonprofit organizations encourage board giving, but CMF's requirement is made explicit for every incoming board member. In addition to financial support, CMF's board members are often in positions to help reach out to potential donors and government partners in China. With "skin in the game" through their financial investment, CMF's board is highly committed and involved with its success in China.

Given the importance of relationships in Asia, it is natural for boards of trustees to further organizations' causes. We also found that for those organizations that begin within the elite, the board offers productive social empowerment. Outside such circles, boards tend to have less reach, and are often comprised of friends and family, when such a board exists at all. Closing this gap of experience can help many SDOs in Asia, as they increase the capacity of their boards to help achieve their missions.

Well-connected: Pre-existing Relationships

Of the 30 Asian SDOs studied, there remain several started by practitioners from outside of business and political circles. Dedicated and resourceful founders have established some of Asia's most prolific nonprofits; but no such success is a solitary affair, as our studies show. Organizations begun by outsiders often receive the help of benefactors encountered on the way to development. Insiders in their respective fields have provided support ranging from financial, or in-kind, to something more akin to *guanxi*, as founders tap into the resources and trust of well-connected friends to bring their ideas to fruition.

Jaime Aristotle Alip did just this in the Philippines, after he founded CARD Mutually Reinforcing Institutions (MRI), a microfinance network, in 1986. Alip was not a member of the elite himself—CARD was famously established with a 20-peso (US$1) bill and a mechanical typewriter for tapping out proposals—but his pre-existing relationships were critical in getting the idea off the ground in the first place. As Alip described it; "Perhaps because of pity, my friend's company accepted my proposal and provided US$10,000."[2] CARD's first donors were acquired through contacts Alip had acquired from his time at the Philippine Business for Social Progress (PBSP), a social development foundation established by a Philippine business consortium. With a little help from his friend—the Japanese foundation Asian Community Trust is a long-time international funder of the PBSP—Alip was able to take the first steps towards fulfilling his vision for a bank owned and managed by landless poor women. Today it has 1 million loans on its ledger and protects 8 million people under its insurance schemes.

Alip didn't stop there, nor did the productive use of his relationships. CARD became a trusted and respected organization, and Alip had become acquainted with Wash SyCip, a successful business leader who provided most of his philanthropy to improve the life chances of poor rural children. Although CARD was a microfinance organization without experience in the education sector, SyCip provided P20 million (US$430,000) for a pilot CARD MRI educational loan program tested in two rural provinces. It succeeded, and the program expanded nationwide. SyCip himself put in US$1 million and through his own network convinced several New York financiers to also offer substantial funding for the further development of the program.

Support from India's business and political elite was also a major driver behind the Council of Environment, Energy and Water (CEEW), an Indian policy think tank. Leaving an illustrious career in international development, Arunabha Ghosh ghostwrote a proposal for a world-class environmental think tank. He shared it with former minister Suresh Prabhu and business leader Jamshyd Godrej, chairman of Godrej & Boyce Manufacturing Company. They not only shared his vision but had been advocating for the establishment of such a research organization for some time. "I was assured that the individuals who would become our board members were seeing the gaps that were resonating with me," said Ghosh. "If they were not there, I wouldn't necessarily have come back to India and started something."

CEEW began operations in August 2010 in a sparsely furnished room in Gurgaon, operating with two staff members and a donation from Godrej of INR 5000 (around US$100 at the time). It is now internationally recognized as one of India's best think tanks and serves as an example of *guanxi* coming full circle, with a multiplying effect. CEEW added to its board of prominent trustees, which now includes business leaders S. Ramadorai, Deepak S. Parekh, and Anil Kakodkar, former chairman of the Atomic Energy Commission. All are active in promoting the organization's research and agenda for an evidence-based approach to sustainable development. In 2015, Prabhu, now minister for railways, released a CEEW policy briefing on the solar potential of Indian railways.

Bypassing the Trust Deficit

Like Wash SyCip, supporters of these SDOs put their faith in personal affiliations they perceived to be trustworthy, transparent and accountable. Such relationships provide a starting point for charity that differs from many places in the West, where donors may seek a particular organization more than a known individual. Relationships matter elsewhere, too, and a well-placed champion is an asset anywhere in the world, but in Asia, a personal connection becomes especially valuable in the absence of due diligence mechanisms.

A trusted domestic broker has the capacity to boost an SDO's credibility. In Thailand, with its complex interaction between business, the military, and the state, the royal family brings unique credibility to public ventures. Revered by the Thai people, the royal family generally stays above the fray of political strife, and are perceived as trustworthy actors in public life. Organizations who receive the royal seal of approval, such as the Foundation for Slum Child Care (FSCC) are accredited with a level of confidence that is beyond reproach in the Thai context. Although the FSCC had already enjoyed an affiliation with the elite and international accolades, royal patronage changed the game for its co-founders, Nongyao Narumitrekakarn and Prateep Ungsontham. Narumitrekakarn, a respected socialite, became aware of the squalid conditions in Klongtoey Slum when her brother worked as an architect on a public project there. While visiting, she met activist Ungsontham who was raised in the slum and had established a "one-baht-a-day" school at her home for the many neighborhood children who did not have access to education. Ungsontham had already had local success. In 1972, she was photographed standing in front of a tractor that had been sent by the Bangkok Metropolitan Authority to demolish the school and reclaim the land. For her efforts to save the school, she was awarded the Ramon Magsaysay Award for Public Service in 1978 and the John D. Rockefeller Youth Award for her "outstanding contribution to mankind" in 1981.

That same year, the two women established FSCC to provide day care for slum children who were left to fend for themselves while their parents worked. Together, the duo caught the eye of HRH Princess Galyani Vadhana Krom Luang Naradhiwas Rajanagarindra, a prolific philanthropist, who was intrigued by a profile in an English-language newspaper, *Bangkok Post*, on a "nursery for the poor." Princess Galyani's patronage of the FSCC was a turning point for the organization, bringing recognition and confidence along with the royal seal of approval. They went on to raise the funds needed to expand operations to other slum districts within Bangkok, and eventually establish a nationwide training network to offer official certification for child care providers.

When SDOs lack direct access to the elite, intermediaries play an important role in connecting deserving organizations with potential benefactors and supporters. In India, where a 2013 Companies Act mandates that 2 percent of after-tax income be directed to corporate social responsibility activities, a number of intermediary organizations have emerged to help businesses and individuals make sense of their giving. Among these are GiveIndia and Guidestar India, online portals that connects donors with screened nonprofits, and Dasra, providing bespoke research and management services to donors while working to build the capacity of recipient organizations. More informal groups in India also act as trusted brokers, such as Caring Friends India, which businessman Ramesh Kacholia founded to "act as a bridge between outstanding NGOs and donors." Over the years, it has identified 30 such NGOs across 10 states in India, one of which is Dilasa Sanstha, a grassroots organization aiming to alleviate the suffering of farmers in drought-prone areas, by providing microcredit and the adaptation of indigenous irrigation systems.

Babu C. Joseph, former chief executive officer of the Axis Bank Foundation, heard of Dilasa Sanstha through Caring Friends. He eventually supported it with a grant of around US$1.8 million, helping more than 8000 farmers and extending credit to 43,000 beneficiaries. Caring Friends is not a registered NGO and has no bank account,[3] but it has built an informal network of Kacholia's friends and supporters who are bound together by a wish to do well. "The common cord that binds them is a genuine desire to reach out to those who need our care," writes Joseph. "The beauty of the association is its simplicity and informality and this friendship has resulted in providing support to several organizations."[4] In this sense, intermediaries such as Caring Friends have successfully leveraged their own *guanxi* to help worthy organizations in India that are deficient in it.

Organizations can also develop helpful relationships by first attracting international recognition. When Dutchman Willie Smits stumbled across Suara Alam, it was an Indonesian grassroots radio station with a mission to highlight local environmental injustices. Smits, an experienced philanthropist, provided it with funds to set up a TV station and get on the radar of international organizations. The group rebranded as Telapak and went on to work directly with local communities to establish sustainable logging cooperatives, creating livelihood options for farmers as opposed to illegal poaching. For this work, it received awards in social entrepreneurship from the Schwab and Skoll foundations, and Telapak president Ambrosius Ruwindrijarto won the prestigious Ramon Magsaysay Award for Emergent Leadership in 2012.

Such accolades have a multiplying effect, attracting donor funding from foreign governments and foundations seeking to get behind a tested organization that meets their strategic objectives in Indonesia. Many of these organizations lacked visibility in Indonesia's nonprofit sector, and Telapak became one of the few trusted names for many international funders in a notoriously opaque sector. This confidence eventually transferred to multinational companies, who turned to Telapak for advice. It now provides advisory services to large corporations operating in the country on how to work with communities in a sustainable way, and in 2014 this income comprised 25 percent of its total revenues. In a country such as Indonesia, which has historically been beset by corruption, international accolades such as those showered on Telapak amount to a form of due diligence where credible actors in the nonprofit sector are otherwise difficult to locate and verify.

Yang Lihe provides another example of how a founder's long-time international connectivity can prove critical to the success of an SDO. Yang, a former village doctor, became a leading researcher on leprosy, working for the Chinese government's main research center and as an advocate for patient rights. He also founded HANDA in 1996, a GONGO (government-operated NGO) providing services treating leprosy in 12 of China's 23 provinces. To support its mission, Yang leveraged the connections of his long career in public health, as a university researcher, and as a government official. While government support made the creation of HANDA possible, it is these additional relationships that have enabled its growth. HANDA's first major donor was the corporate foundation of Novartis, the Swiss pharmaceutical company, and international sponsors remain its lifeblood today, providing 73 percent of HANDA's income in 2014.

In a broad sense, relationships offer Asians a way around lack of trust in the system. In nations where regulators do not require transparency or accountability, donors need other sorts of reassurance that their money will be well spent. Traditionally, personal networks have filled that gap. Today, new means to conduct due diligence have entered the marketplace through the use of technology, and such technology is helping organizations take on roles of trusted advisors, allowing people to sustain communities where none had existed before.

Indonesia offers a prime example of technology empowering new relationships. They have been crucial to the success of the Academy of Sharing, Akademi Berbagi in the Bahasa, a national social movement for skill training with media personalities and business leaders offering free face-to-face classes for young people. It began with a tweet: when founder and PR consultant Ainun Chomsun went online in search of career information, she sent a public message over Twitter to Subiakto Priosoedarsono, founder of one of Indonesia's top advertising firms, soliciting his advice.

> "I want to learn to be a copywriter, Mr. Bi, tell me how?" she tweeted.
>
> "I teach, you interested?" Subiakto tweeted back a few minutes later.

The exchange cumulated in him offering to teach a free class at his office to a small group, for which word spread quickly over social media. Dozens of aspiring copywriters attended. The movement for free-of-charge skills training grew, with teachers drawn from Indonesian business and media. Through social media, Akademi Berbagi had blossomed into a national public platform open to all for learning and sharing with experts, with classes coordinated online and conducted offline. Since that first copywriting class in 2010, 30,000 students have attended some 1000 classes, which were led by 200 teachers assisted by an equal number of volunteers. Twitter provided an open platform for the genesis of Akademi Berbagi, requiring the organization to be an open, transparent operation. Its success offers a new way for SDOs to think about how to leverage the public forum provided by social media to build trust in lieu of pre-existing *guanxi*.

Throughout Asia, there are more and more initiatives applying technology to enhance transparency and gain trust. In Hong Kong, WiseGiving is an online platform allowing potential donors to look under the hood of Hong Kong-based SDOs to see how each organization spends the funds it raises. In Singapore, the National Philanthropy and Volunteer Center is a government-backed agency aiming to improve efficacy and transparency of SDOs while aiding philanthropists to make informed decisions. They too have constructed an online platform to facilitate this process.

Throughout Asia, the rise of social media has also empowered and enabled the citizen watchdog movement, curtailing those trying to exploit the system or engage in fraud. While these efforts are still in their early days, the trajectory of the trend is clear. Citizens are creating alternative mechanisms to fund and oversee social development initiatives with and without the inclusion of the traditional elite.

Conclusions: Strategies for *Guanxi* in the Social Delivery Sector

Guanxi persists as a currency of trust in the social delivery sector, rooted in the context of community and family in Asia and bolstered by weak regulatory environments and a resulting dearth of trust. New organizations face barriers to financing and support, given wariness on the part of philanthropists and donors toward homegrown institutions. "Donations can be made only when these fundamentals [infrastructure, legal system and human resources] are all in place," said Chinese philanthropist and founder of Alibaba, Jack Ma. "That's why I think giving donations to charities is more difficult than earning money," he said.[5]

In this context, founders from or close to the elite of society have been best positioned to achieve success across the 30 SDOs studied. Fong of Lifeline Express and Lien of Lien AID were able to leverage their considerable personal resources to move their own projects ahead. Meanwhile, Alip of CARD MRI and Ghosh of CEEW benefited from their insider status acquired from years of building relationships and providing advice as national experts in their respective fields. On the surface, these observations would be disheartening for less well-connected, aspiring SDO founders with bright ideas. But SDOs within the study have deployed various other tactics to garner credibility and gain access to funding and resources.

Other methods of maximizing relationships include:

Seek alternative accreditation: Soliciting international recognition gave Telapak credibility to attract funding and raise its profile, especially among international funding agencies looking to expand their activities in Indonesia. Co-founder Ungsontham's international profile as a slum activist similarly drew attention from international donors to FSCC, but it was royal patronage that ensured its domestic longevity. Getting on the radar of international organizations, including those highlighting the work of high-performing SDOs, can serve as a fillip to future prospects. But whether this strategy is viable for an SDO depends highly on their aspirations and the local context.

Cultivate relationships with intermediary organizations: In India, where nonprofits have to register under the Foreign Contribution Regulation Act to receive funds from overseas, aspiring to recognition among international supporters might not be a viable strategy. In such cases, intermediary organizations can connect donors and nonprofits, and there are many in India as a result of the regulatory environment. Organizations such as Dasra, Guidestar India and GiveIndia offer a clearinghouse function by vetting charities and helping them develop positive relationships with engaged donors.

Many such intermediaries actively help SDOs build confidence among donors by developing their internal skills in management, financials, and operations. They also have created optional accreditation systems to help SDOs improve their appeal to donors. The China Social Entrepreneur Foundation (You Change) is currently rolling out a system assessing social entrepreneurs by a number of metrics to become certified by You Change. WiseGiving and NVPC have already established platforms to aid worthy organizations.

Focus online: The case of Akademi Berbagi is an unusual one: few organizations were born on the basis of a tweet. However, it does illustrate the extent to which the operating environment has changed for SDOs, offering new ways in which they can take advantage of changing dynamics. SDOs can directly engage with debate and even shape the discussion of philanthropy through social media, using its platforms to build up credibility with the public. Already, organizations such as Give India are following in the footsteps of Guidestar in the United States and Europe, using an open-source database for organizational data, allowing donors to make their own assessments. Information availability and data is much patchier in Asia, with its inconsistent reporting requirements and varying attitudes toward transparency, but if the case of Akademi Berbagi is anything to go by, those organizations able to harness the Internet improve their chances of thriving.

These strategies, alone or in combination, can help an SDO work around a shortfall of *guanxi*, a lack of access to elite resources and support. Leveraging relationships in some manner will be crucial for a new organization, as it has been for each of the SDOs studied across Asia. For many of them, pre-existing relationships played a critical role, either through founders who were well placed to draw upon trusted relationships with members of the elite or by those founded by a member of the elite themselves, investing their own resources and relationships to the benefit of the SDO. Others found their way to productive relationships through outside accolades or assistance, or through social media.

In none of those cases do relationships provide all that organizations need. They must still work at building transparency, accountability, and impact measurement, especially in Asia, where the trust deficit remains as a legacy of an unclear regulatory environment. Registration and reporting requirements vary, but in many places, these appear to be insufficient to gain the trust of donors and supporters without the credibility brought by *guanxi*.

Notes

1. Witt, Michael A. and Gordon Redding. *The Oxford Handbook of Asian Business Systems*. Oxford University Press, Oxford, UK, 2015.
2. "CARD MRI, An Example of Microfinance Success." Asian Institute of Finance, Manila, Philippines, 2013.
3. Dutta, Anirudha. "The Power of One." *Forbes India Blog*, July 2, 2013. http://www.forbesindia.com/blog/beyond-the-numbers/corporate-india-and-csr/. Accessed June 21, 2016.
4. Caring Friends: Helping Good NGOs Perform Better, Mumbai, India. https://sites.google.com/a/caringfriends.in/caring-friends/testimonials. Accessed June 21, 2016.
5. http://www.scmp.com/news/china/money-wealth/article/1858697/its-harder-donate-money-chinese-charities-earn-it-says. Accessed September 16, 2015.

CHAPTER 6

Government, Here to Help!

Manisha Mirchandani

When Yao Li sought to set up a free-of-charge vocational education school for the children of migrant workers in Beijing, she had the ideal background for the challenge. A prominent Chinese businesswoman, she tapped into her extensive network of contacts to garner support for Bainian Vocational School (BNVS). It now comprises nine branches in major Chinese cities plus an international branch in the capital of Angola, all under the direction of an illustrious board assembled by Yao Li, including former housing adviser to the Hong Kong government Simon Li, and well-known media personality and former CCTV journalist Wang Jie.

But it was a fortuitous meeting with the China Youth Development Foundation (CYDF) that cemented the launch of BNVS and its eventual success. CYDF, one of the country's oldest and largest national public foundations, has a particularly important network. With this partnership as a foundation, BNVS was able to succeed in spectacular fashion. Around 2500 underprivileged young people from across China graduated from its programs from 2005 to 2015, trained as skilled workers.[1]

CYDF's clout means that it plays an important role in setting the national youth development agenda, one amplifying the reach of its graduates and personnel. Founded by the All China Youth Federation, it was the driving force behind Project Hope, a national initiative that had sup-

M. Mirchandani
CAPS, Hong Kong SAR, China

R.A. Shapiro et al., *Pragmatic Philanthropy*,
https://doi.org/10.1007/978-981-10-7119-5_6

ported 5 million students in rural areas to continue their education by 2013. As a partner, CYDF could offer Yao Li not just experience but prominence and broad approval. Tu Meng, then vice chairperson and secretary general of CYDF, knew Yao Li faced a challenging maze of laws and regulations to establish a nonprofit school if she pursued them alone. "What you are missing, we have it all," he told her.

Reimagining the Social Contract

Tu and Yao Li soon reached an agreement whereby CYDF would subsidize BNVS from its own Vocational Education Fund. And through this affiliation with CYDF, BNVS could now undertake public fundraising, which was to prove a crucial factor in its development and future growth.

Their partnership reflected currents in the country as a whole. Their initial discussions took place amid a long-term shift in how the Chinese government viewed the social sector's developmental role. In the past, the majority of social services, and practically all education services, were provided by the state. That began to change in the 1990s, as China began a process of economic reform that included considering different approaches for public service delivery.

In China, the practice of procuring nonprofit contractors to deliver education and health care services on behalf of the state is not as well established as in some other countries. As Beijing began collaborating with both the private sector and social organizations to explore new models of service delivery, CYDF was at the forefront of this movement in education. It would be a critical partner in piloting the BNVS model for vocational schooling.

This offered a pathway for migrant children unable to access the formal education system due to strict residency requirements while also responding to a growing demand in China's labor market for more service-oriented, technically skilled workers. Perhaps drawing inspiration from the success of the BNVS, the government has since announced plans to increase the number of vocational education schools countrywide, with a target of providing universal free-of-charge training.

This shift in public-sector thinking is not limited to China. Governments across Asia have become increasingly open to new ways of financing and delivering on public expectations as the social contract forged with their citizens comes under increasing strain. In the wave of postwar independence, new governments across the region had attempted to bring together fragmented and diverse societies through a unifying vision, as exemplified through Jawaharlal Nehru's interconnected India, and

Sukarno's harmonizing *Pancasila* principles in Indonesia. In other countries, the contract that was brokered was more transactional, with the promise of public services and prosperity in exchange for social stability. From Lee Kuan Yew's Singapore to Mahathir's Malaysia to Deng Xiao Peng's modern China, this deal helped to foster the stability required for East Asia's economic ascent.

In the more developed economies of the region, traditional pathways to social mobility are becoming closed off. A new generation is no longer seeing sufficient returns on acquiescence and are demanding a greater voice in decision-making. The student-led Umbrella Movement of Hong Kong in 2014 demanded broader representation in selection of its leaders, and opposition parties in Singapore rose on the support of young people via social media channels. In the developing countries of Asia, many with large, young populations, governments are under pressure to raise living standards and provide jobs to quell discontent—for example, Indonesia's youth unemployment rates remain worryingly high at 21 percent, according to World Bank data. This is all taking place in the wake of the 2008 global financial crisis and subsequent economic shocks, when fiscal pressures on the public purse have never been greater.

For Service Delivery

Amid this changing social dynamic in Asia, domestic social delivery organizations (SDOs) are emerging to play a more prolific role in public service delivery. Multilateral development agencies encourage collaborative models of partnership between the government and non-traditional actors in the delivery of health care, education, poverty alleviation, and environmental services. It has not always been so: SDOs in Asia have not historically been so broadly interested in collaboration models. But now, partnership with government has become all but essential to achieving their aims. Across the 30 nonprofits and social enterprises studied, there are few exceptions to this rule. A closer look at the high performers in their countries shows us various ways to partner with government across the region, collaboration taking place at different phases in the evolution of the SDO. Indeed, the arrangements being struck are as diverse as the countries of Asia themselves.

The most straightforward means by which to work with government is to be contracted by government to carry out social delivery services. Of the 15 economies in our Doing Good Index study, all allow for the procurement of services of SDOs to deliver social goods, although six go further and add incentives for SDOs to compete for government contracts.

In fact, in Hong Kong, of the 450 SDOs listed with the Hong Kong Council of Social Services Wise Giving platform, 49 percent of their aggregated budgets come from government contracts, the highest among the countries we studied. As noted in Chapter 2, there are historical reasons for this. In economies where colonialism played a formative role, the government simply did not have the desire or bandwidth to carry out social delivery functions. They contracted out these tasks to local groups. In the case of Hong Kong, this practice continues today through government procurement schemes.

Although the enthusiasm for working with government partners varies depending on domestic dynamics, direct engagement with government is broadly necessary at some stage for SDOs to thrive. As our case studies indicate, there comes a time when the founder or manager will likely reflect on how it will forge its relationship with relevant government entities. More often than not, it is not a case of considering *why* they should work with government but usually a matter of *when* and *how*.

As JV Partners

To achieve their objectives, some SDOs were established with an understanding that they would need to partner with government to even make it onto the playing field. Recognizing the value of this form of endorsement, such "joint ventures" (JVs) are sought willingly by SDO founders.

The joint venture struck between Yao Li and Tu Meng was critical to the BNVS concept even getting off the ground. Right at the start, domestic fundraising posed a major barrier to BNVS' efforts, which required government authorization for nonprofit schools. Through its affiliation with CYDF, BNVS was able to fundraise within Mainland China, eventually coming to depend almost exclusively on domestic funding. By the 2013–2014 school year, 86 percent of its income came from domestic sources, rising to 93 percent the next year. In addition, BNVS benefited from free-of-charge usage of CYDF premises—classrooms for the Zhengzhou school were provided by the Henan Communist Youth League, a CYDF member. The CYDF connection has also been helpful in recruiting for BNVS, a virtual unknown in its early days, enabling it to attract the teaching capacity required for its schools to run.

Through CYDF, the government has remained a controlling stakeholder and interested observer of Yao Li's experimental model. Tu Meng, also a BNVS board member, acted as an important conduit between government and BNVS while providing a lens for BNVS into the government's plans for the vocational sector and youth development. But most critical to Yao Li's success has been the official seal of approval stamp BNVS received by its partnership with the government-affiliated CYDF, which Tu described as a "successful innovation."

In Malaysia, we found a much more explicit arrangement struck between the government and the Sports Racquet Association of Malaysia (SRAM). Established in the 1972 by young Malays and expatriates who played the game at exclusive clubs in Kuala Lumpur, SRAM's founding purpose was to popularize the game of squash in Malaysia. Its major benefactor today, the National Sports Council (NSC) of the Ministry of Youth and Sports, began supporting the association in the 1990s in the wake of Malaysia's winning bid for the 1998 Commonwealth Games. The government threw its support behind SRAM and other sports groups in a bid to help the nation's athletes win prestige for Malaysia, spending more than US$468 million on the games. SRAM worked primarily at the state level, building facilities, recruiting young athletes, and developing a world-class training program.

In addition to financial support, the government also intervened to connect SRAM to sources of corporate funding. In 1995, the Ministry of Youth and Sports introduced a program known as *Rakan Sukan* (sports partner) to encourage Malaysian corporations to adopt a sport and provide the requisite financial assistance and management training to help elevate it to international standards. Industry responded to the call, and SRAM was matched with YTL Corporation Berhad, a Malaysian infrastructure conglomerate founded by business tycoon Francis Yeoh Tiong Lay. From 1996 to 2003, YTL contributed US$1.3 million, until the baton was subsequently taken up by Nazir Razak, squash player and chief executive officer of CIMB Bank, who remained a primary corporate sponsor for SRAM till 2015.

Through the NSC, the government continues to be the biggest sponsor of SRAM's programs and its athletes, providing 56 percent of its total funds in 2014. As a direct investor, the government was in essence funding SRAM as an extension of the national sports program, an approach possible only given the perfect alignment of their objectives to elevate squash as a national sport. SRAM's founding vision to democratize squash and develop world-class players aligned perfectly with that of the Malaysian government seeking to raise the country's global sporting image. SRAM was perceived to be an effective vehicle with the expertise and networks to develop sporting talent at the grassroots level—where a Malaysian superstar was discovered. International sporting icon Nicol David, who has won the World Squash Open a record-breaking eight times, is a shining example of this joint venture's success.

As Venture Funders

Public grants and subsidies now give Asia's social sector access to funds long available for economic development. Historically, governments of the region have utilized subsidies to support the growth of strategic sectors, including the electronics industry in Japan, South Korea, and Taiwan. This concept is now trickling through the social sector, as governments redirect subsidies toward new growth areas, such as renewable energy and environmental services. The social enterprises in our study have benefited from this pivot by capitalizing upon new procurement opportunities that have arisen from Asian governments eager to develop their green economies.

Building a social enterprise around tree planting was very much a blue-sky idea for Tree Planet co-founder Jeong Mincheol. But rather than join a nonprofit that specialized in reforestation, Jeong wanted to prove that it was possible to build a profitable business that could also have a real environmental impact. Noting the Korean government's Green Growth policy agenda and the support that was being made available to industry, Jeong and his co-founder Kim Hyungsoo went to the market with an idea for selling customized replanting projects to consumers.

With the demand for environmentally minded products and services being stimulated, Tree Planet was able to thrive as a profitable business, with revenues of close to US$1 million in 2015. Alongside the K-pop fans who pay Tree Planet to plant and personalize forestry projects dedicated to their idols, the Seoul Metropolitan Government has been a consistent client of the organization in urban replanting initiatives.

Green growth is also blooming in China. Since the Chinese government prioritized the green economy within its 12th Five-Year Plan for 2011–2015, government agencies right down to the municipal level have received significant financial support to put toward environmental spending. This has paid off for social enterprise Landwasher, the developer of an environmental toilet that can save an estimated 2.2 tons of water and around 7300 kilowatt hours of electricity a year compared to a traditional portable model. Now with assets of US$10 million, Landwasher has installed more than 10,000 of its toilets across the country, making it China's top waterless toilet-solution provider.

Deciding that the concept of a social enterprise was still confusing to the domestic Chinese market, Wu prefers to call his company an "environmental enterprise," as the term is less likely to be associated with sensitive nonprofit activities in the Chinese non-governmental sector. It also directly links his proposition to funding earmarked for "green" solutions, helping him open doors to government agencies such as the tourism bureaus and local development departments that remain Landwasher's client base. Its core business is in installing mobile toilets in remote tourist areas and municipal areas off the grid from urban sanitation and sewer systems. Its big breakthrough came in 2008, when it was selected from more than 200 bidders to supply water-free toilets for the Olympic Games in Beijing. From there on, it has been the supplier of choice for other premium large-scale events in China, such as the 60th Anniversary Celebration of the People's Republic of China, for which it provided 350 movable toilets.

Government subsidies have also benefited Landwasher in less direct ways. Local government agencies have played an important role in supporting Landwasher's development. Its classification as a high-tech enterprise means that it is eligible for tax and financing benefits and other forms of enterprise support from the Langfang, Hebei Province authorities. But primarily, Landwasher interacts with government agencies as a preferred vendor. Public-sector contracts remain the bread and butter of its business, to the extent that Wu categorizes his company as being in the "business-to-government" sector.

Getting buy-in from government actors was a similar factor in the success of the Center for Agriculture and Rural Development (CARD), a Filipino social enterprise. Established in 1986, CARD has developed a network of "Mutually Reinforcing Institutions" (MRI) to extend access to financial services to the rural poor. The CARD MRI network reaches far and deep into several provinces in the Philippines, a nation of 100 million, of whom an estimated 25 percent are considered poor. CARD has been extremely successful with more than one million loans and 8 million insurance customers.

Its engagement with government kicked in when the organization's founder, Jaime Aristotle Alip, sought to take CARD to the next level in 1995. CARD's loan portfolio had already grown from 200 borrowers in 1988 to 4240 through the implementation of a microfinance group lending model. But Alip wanted to do more; he had a vision of creating Philippines' first microfinance bank to be managed and partly owned by up to 1 million poor members. Upon being granted a license by the Philippines Central Bank, CARD Bank was established in September 1997.

In growing its network of MRIs, CARD increasingly worked with relevant branches of the Philippines national government, including the Central Bank, the Insurance Commission, and the Securities and Exchange Commission (SEC), to facilitate conditions conducive to the proliferation of microfinance. With the SEC, it developed commercial notes, a short-term debt instrument for corporations, for microfinance clients. CARD MRI's lobbying efforts led to changes in law that officially recognized microfinance as a legitimate form of banking in 2000. This has set the stage for the sector's growth since then, and the implementation of microfinance-based models for a wide range of services and products.

CARD MRI's reach now extends beyond financial services. In 2012, it hosted a summit on the link between poverty and health, which resulted in an agreement to push for national reform. CARD's own business activities have contributed to a dramatic increase in the number of people covered by micro insurance services; by 2010, about 21 percent of insured Filipinos received insurance through one of its MRIs. To achieve CARD MRI's ultimate goal of making financial services widely available and affordable for the rural poor, they had to engage with government at the very highest levels, acquiring the necessary operating licenses and driving the policy changes necessary for the microfinance sector to take root and grow.

As Hybrid

When working with nonprofits, Asian governments incline toward grant-giving. As noted, more than 50 percent of some SDOs' budgets come from government contracts. This dependency poses a concern for some founders and managers, whose revenues are vulnerable to changes in administration or government spending priorities.

As will also be discussed in Chapter 8, alternative models are on the rise. In Taiwan, Eden Welfare Foundation (EWF), whose revenues amounted to around US$40 million in 2014, has shifted. Historically dependent on government funding and recognizing the need for a more sustainable income stream, the organization has recently focused on developing income from its social enterprise arm. It now contracts out trained disabled workers to provide cleaning, baking and other services to private-sector and government clients.

In Hong Kong, the Haven of Hope Christian Service (HoH) also diversified. For years, HoH has received public funding to deliver essential health care services to the population under the Hospital Authority. With a staff of over 2000, this faith-based nonprofit provides integrated medical and social services at 46 locations, serving some 100,000 people since it was founded in the 1950s by missionaries. In 2012–2013 it received 51 percent of its US$55 million budget from the Hong Kong government, with the rest from a combination of fundraising, donations, grants, and investment returns.

The challenge for the Haven of Hope is to strike a balance between serving the health care needs of the community while staying true to its founding mission and values. It has done so by directing its self-generated funds toward activities that align with its spiritual values that are not covered in its public remit. One such area is palliative care services, for which there is a dearth of facilities in Hong Kong, which lagged behind Taiwan, Singapore, Japan, and South Korea in the Quality of Death Index, the Economist Intelligence Unit's 2015 assessment of end-of-life care. Seeking to fill this gap, Haven of Hope established the Sister Annie Skau Holistic Care Center in 2006 to care for the mind, body, and spirit of the terminally ill, directing resources where the health care system was unable or unwilling. Today, the center runs itself on a social enterprise model, relying on donations for only 15 percent of its expenditure.

Hong Chi Association has also been a long-time beneficiary of Hong Kong government grants, which amounted to US$70 million for the 2014–2015 financial year. It has embarked on a pilot project in which it hopes to forge a new sort of procurement relationship. Established in 1965 to provide educational services to the mentally handicapped, Hong Chi Association sends people with intellectual disabilities to collect used glass bottles and process them for the production of eco-bricks. In the first of its kind project funded by the charitable arm of the Hong Kong Jockey Club, Hong Chi Association is working closely with the Environmental Protection Department in the hope that by 2018, it will be hired as a preferred vendor for the government's glass recycling scheme.

For Policy Change

As nearly all of our case studies indicate, government partnerships across the region follow a spirit of pragmatism. When it comes to social delivery, the organizations studied show signs that they are less inclined toward changing the status quo and more interested in solving a problem at hand; two-thirds focus entirely on creating a direct impact for their beneficiaries, with no agenda or inclination to participate in the policy discourse. For the vast majority of Asian SDOs, maximizing the number of people whose lives have been improved is the self-purported goal.

When they do seek policy change in the interests of their beneficiaries—be it to champion the rights of disabled people in Taiwan in the case of Eden Welfare Foundation, or to improve public benefits for the elderly in Japan as was the mission for Sawayaka Well-being Foundation—they tend to do so through a collaborative approach, as opposed to adversarial. This manifests itself in organizations that begin life in an advisory capacity. Founders are typically respected thinkers or practitioners with existing cache within the country, and often abroad. Whether they be from within the establishment or having worked with friendly international entities, they have come from a background where they have worked with or on behalf of government entities. They have created these new organizations not to challenge the status quo, but to provide expertise and the knowhow to help move it along.

As National Expert

The founder of Coral Triangle Center (CTC), an Indonesian organization at the forefront of domestic efforts to drive sustainable use of marine resources, is one case in point. Rili Djohani worked for the World Wildlife Fund in developing its marine conservation portfolio and joined the Indonesian branch of The Nature Conservancy to help establish its coastal and marine programs, including one in Bali. From 2004 to 2008 she was TNC's country director for Indonesia with responsibility for forest and coastal management.

However, international NGOs in Indonesia cannot raise money inside the country, which for Djohani limited their ability to be self-sufficient and truly responsive to domestic needs. With the support of prominent backers with a concern for the environment, the Coral Triangle Center headquartered in Bali was established. Indonesian businessman George Tahija and diplomat and government veteran Hasyim Djalal were founding directors, alongside Made Subadia, a top Indonesian conservation official.

Djohani's expertise and ability to represent domestic interests in international circles quickly raised CTC's profile as the national authority on issues of marine conservation. CTC is the only domestic partner involved in the Coral Triangle Initiative, a formal pact by the six nations that flank the beautiful Coral Triangle waters—waters highly vulnerable to ecosystem damage. The other seven conservation partners selected are from the major international agencies that Djohani used to work for and with. CTC is also well placed to communicate directly with the government on such matters of ocean governance, with two board members who represent the Indonesian government on maritime and external affairs.

For Arunabha Ghosh, getting the ear of policymakers was initially a tricky task, but one that he believed was critical in the face of India's looming environmental crisis. As a respected global thinker on climate governance, Ghosh had previously worked at the World Trade Organization, the United Nations Development Program, and as an author of the annual Human Development Report. He became increasingly concerned with the paucity of data and information available to Indian policymakers on issues of sustainable development. In 2010, this drove him to accept a challenge from business and policy leaders in India and build an independent research organization, the Council for Environment, Energy and Water (CEEW).

Going against the grain of India's traditionally noisy advocacy groups, CEEW seeks to affect policy change on the strength of its research and the evidence it generates. With the support of prominent Indian business leaders, and importantly, a board co-chairman in former Union-level minister for environment and forests, fertilizers and power, and heavy industry and public enterprises Suresh Prabhu, Ghosh and his research team aspired to provide the data that policymakers required to make well-informed decisions on important issues of resource management and environmental governance.

Although it was conceived first and foremost to fill a vacuum for reliable empirical data on policy issues, engaging with government has been one of the more difficult aspects of CEEW's mission. "It is hard to get access to government in Asia, and no one is going to compliment you or even acknowledge your work at times. It can be like selling yourself from scratch, every time," said Ghosh. But CEEW has continued to parlay its expertise in government circles and developed a much deeper engagement over the years.

The appointment of Prabhu as minister of railways under the new National Democratic Alliance government in 2014 has now also provided CEEW with a direct line into the Indian government at the highest levels. With its growing caché and largely on the strength and relevance of its original data and research, CEEW has been invited to advise government on more than 140 occasions, both in India and abroad.

In politically volatile Thailand, the Foundation for Slum Child Care's (FSCC) was established in 1981 in part to fill what its founders viewed as a failure of the public welfare system. Public childcare for those under the age of two is not available in Thailand. The shortfalls of this were most evident in Bangkok's slums in the 1980s, where a generation of babies and young children was born into miserable conditions while lacking adequate care and supervision. FSCC came under the royal patronage of the late HRH Princess Galyani Vadhana and become a reputable provider of childcare services and professional training, caring for 2133 young children in 2014.

Although its raison d'etre was to plug gaps in social service provision that the government was not inclined to fill, FSCC eventually would take a more strategic approach, like CARD-MRI, to circumvent what it saw as bad policy. The requirements for childcare providers to register with the Ministry of Social Development and Human Security were so onerous that the vast majority of centers were unable to meet them. This encouraged an unregulated grey sector for childcare, leaving large numbers of children vulnerable to mistreatment.

So FSCC brokered a deal with the government. Through its community networks, it would recruit unregistered community-level childcare centers, and provide proprietors with professional training under its Network for Childcare Services Co-development scheme. Those who passed the course received an FSCC certification, and with this they would be able to register formally with the ministry. FSCC's royal pedigree and professional reputation made it a trusted partner in the eyes of both government actors and informal operators. And it came with a good proposal, approaching the government with a solution that precluded the need for policy reform—a challenging task at a time when Thailand's political environment is so in flux. The government agreed. As of 2014, 81 childcare centers from 67 communities within Bangkok had been trained by the FSCC under this program.

As Bellwether

More than in other East Asian nations, civil society in South Korea has been a consistent channel for questioning and challenging political repression.

Against this backdrop, World Without Worries for Shadow Education (WWW), a group seeking to effect change in South Korea's education policy, operates in a more confrontational fashion than either CTC or CEEW but with a comparable emphasis on research and data to inform their conversations with the government. Like protesting farmers, Song In-soo had no qualms about deploying attention-grabbing tactics as part of his organization's efforts to reform the education system. He saw that it was placing enormous pressure on Korean students desperate to beat their competitors for one of a handful of seats at its elite universities. This manifested in the form of a "shadow" industry of cram schools, which Korean parents were willing to invest in to ensure the success of their children, sometimes to the detriment of their mental health. In a worrying 2011 report, the National Teachers Labor Union reported that student suicidal impulses were primarily the result of too much time in cram schools and a fear of poor marks.

Former educator Song established the Citizens' Ministry of Education under WWW with a mission to address the worries of desperate parents who were concerned for the well-being of their children but also scared of them losing their edge in the fierce competition for university places. The Citizen's Ministry compiled data and conducted research to inform its case for the reform of pre-university education, finding that the bar for English language ability for the high school admissions test had been set too high. This gave those who were able to pay for additional tutoring or cram school preparation an unfair advantage. In 2009, the Ministry of Education lowered English language proficiency levels of the tests, causing some cram schools to close—household spending on shadow education dropped for the first time in 20 years.

The Citizen's Ministry ramped up its efforts in 2012, when WWW members staged one-person protests over 100 days in a public open space known as Gwanghwamun in central Seoul, wearing signs urging passersby to support education reform. Recognizing a shift in public sentiment around this issue, political leaders had even sought to promote these reforms in collaboration with WWW. But wary of appearing too close to the fray, WWW maintained its independence with its efforts contributing to the passage of a national law regulating shadow education activities within the public school system. Unlike CTC in Indonesia or CEEW in India, WWW did not seek to co-opt government to effect change, but instead focused its efforts on changing public perceptions and building an evidence-based case for reform that it could take to legislators.

To Scale

Scale is a clear driver for such increased engagement. Many Asian governments have a governance infrastructure that runs right down to the township and village levels, where the local representative acts as the gateway to serving local communities. This is particularly true in the larger democratic nations of India, Indonesia, and the Philippines, where responsibility for public service provision tends to be more decentralized and devolved to officials at the sub-national levels. In fact, even when avoiding national government, many of the SDOs in our study developed relationships with the local government to ease the path to operating in new areas even if their initial instinct is to give wide berth to bureaucracy. Some organizations spoke of conceding agility when it comes to entering into arrangements with governments, who can either be a hindrance or help on the ground.

This was certainly the case for Magic Bus, an Indian youth development charity that began life as an informal club of adults teaching poor youngsters to play rugby. It grew into an organization that helps 300,000 children and teens through a network of 8000 mentors. When founder Matthew Spacie wanted to scale up their efforts nationally, he knew he had to approach the government in order to do so. "The first conversations we had with the government were very difficult, because we learned very quickly that you can't speak to the government unless you have some quantum of scale," he said of his initial outreach to the government. "We withdrew from conversations until we felt we had some firepower to have influence."

Magic Bus was awarded a UNICEF grant of US$120,000 to expand coverage to 150,000 young people, up from the 4500 it was serving at the time. For the Indian government, the grant was a clear signal of Magic Bus's credibility as a potential partner. As Spacie and his team were devising their expansion plan in 2008, the central government launched its Village Youth Sport and Play Initiative. It was India's first initiative by the Ministry of Youth Affairs and Sports to promote social and physical development of rural youth, through which the government provided funds for the development and maintenance of sports grounds at the village level.

In 2010, the national government selected Magic Bus as a partner to implement centers for its new initiative in Maharashtra and Andhra Pradesh states. This was an opportunity for Magic Bus to establish itself to public officials as an effective partner for scaling up the ambitious scheme, instilling trust that it was a pair of safe hands for the job. To this end, when Magic Bus won the World Bank Development Marketplace Prize and received a US$70,000 grant, Spacie spent the money on the measurement and evaluation of existing programs. This evidence of its impact imparted Magic Bus with the confidence it would need to earn the trust of government partners seeking the most effective organizations to work with.

Some SDOs know from the start that they will need to engage with government at a certain point of development. Dr. Armida Fernandez made that choice quite deliberately for the Society for Nutrition, Education & Health Action (SNEHA), which she had established in 1999. Her prior experience of working in a hospital in Mumbai's Dharavi slum showed her that it was not possible to drive significant change through delivery of health care services alone. Only arming Dharavi's residents with the knowledge to help themselves would prevent them from returning to hospital again and again, straining the public health system.

She set up SNEHA with the intention of changing attitudes among slum dwellers and literally bringing health care to the community. As of 2015, it had made 4500 home visits to pregnant women and assisted more than 21,000 women with potential birth complications. It had also monitored the growth of nearly 24,000 children under three years of age in Dharavi, brought health care education to more than 10,000 children and adolescents, and intervened in more than 5000 incidents of violence against women and children. But Dr. Fernandez and her team thought it could achieve an even more lasting impact, by helping to build the capacity of the overstretched public health systems.

An opportunity to collaborate with government emerged from the City Initiative for Newborn Health (CINH), which was formed in partnership with the Municipal Corporation of Greater Mumbai, the public authority responsible for the Mumbai metropolis and suburban areas. CINH was tasked to reduce maternal and neonatal mortality in eight Mumbai wards and to assist some 283,000 people by developing systems for coordination between different levels of administration at the hospitals and clinics—a daunting task in a city of that scale.

Cognizant of how difficult it could be for NGOs to navigate India's bureaucracies and overcome inertia, the SNEHA leaders saw their role within this initiative as that of facilitator and moderator, helping to create an environment that was conducive to cooperation between the various stakeholders. At the first meeting of all those involved, Dr. Fernandez surprised many in the room by opening with praise of government health officials for their accomplishments. She acknowledged the difficulties government workers faced in their jobs, the constraints they faced, and their desire to make a positive difference to the communities they served.

This appreciative opening set the scene for CINH's approach, and it became the country's largest urban health initiative for maternal and newborn health. SNEHA worked with government counterparts to implement standardized clinical protocols and benchmarks at every tier of Mumbai's public health care system. Lines of communication were established between government hospitals, and standards were set for the transfer and tracking of patient cases between and within institutions. Data collection and analysis provided the government actors with rationales for action. When SNEHA examined government data to design the CINH program, it found mismatches between capacity and patient flows, leading to a re-examination of staffing capacity across facilities.

By creating a congenial environment that fostered collaboration between government and non-government actors, SNEHA helped overcome some of the friction associated with bureaucracy. Today, most of SNEHA's programs involve some level of contact with local government agencies, either through delivery of services or in its advocacy efforts. As of 2015, it has trained more than 3000 public health care providers and 2900 government outreach workers.

Conclusion: Strategies for Government Engagement

Successful SDOs collaborate with governments in a variety of ways across Asia. In China, BNVS saw that the endorsement by CYDF gave it legitimacy, making donors feel safe in following the support of Beijing. In Malaysia, SRAM's objectives aligned so perfectly with those of the government that they came together in a marriage of convenience, where SRAM did the work of cultivating sporting talent from the ground up while the government channeled resources from top down. In India, CEEW shared its data with officials, improving their ability to make well-informed decisions.

Each of the social enterprises studied found government as a lucrative client, helping these firms to extend their reach and impact. This was particularly true for environmental-minded enterprises Landwasher and Tree Planet, which have benefited from government not only as consumers of their offerings, but also indirectly as recipients of resources officially channeled to growing the green economy in China and South Asia.

For those nonprofits reliant on government grants, strained public finances have prompted new models of funding. Some have established income-producing social enterprise arms. Eden Welfare Foundation in Taiwan and Hong Chi in Hong Kong now provide training and jobs for the disadvantaged with the view toward improving self-sufficiency of beneficiaries and the organizations themselves. This shift is consistent with the Wang Dao philosophy of philanthropy espoused by Taiwanese industrialist

Stan Shih, who writes of the societal benefits reaped from doing well by doing good.

Only a handful of the SDOs studied had overt aspirations to change the policy environment for their chosen field, and even so, they chose to work with government cooperatively to fill gaps in technical expertise. With accumulated expertise from many years working in established international conservation groups, CTC's Djohani can assist with Indonesia's domestic priorities and provide direct advice to the government on how to better manage their ocean resources. Ghosh initially collaborated to gain access to policymakers, who now recognize the value of CEEW's independent, robust research in informing environmental policymaking. WWW's less-accommodating stance to partnering with government was specific to South Korea's noisy tradition of civil society process, but it still served as a useful bellwether for legislators to understand the shifting national mindset on education reform.

And as frustrating as it can be to engage with government bureaucracy, maturing SDOs recognize this as the only pathway to ramping up the impact of their efforts. Magic Bus gained the trust of government and has been able to expand its reach to 22 of India's 29 states through the national rural sports program. SNEHA realized that strengthening of the public health care system was the only way to drive better outcomes at scale, and to do this Dr. Fernandez fostered collaborative relationships between stakeholders. Inspired by the growth of the microfinance industry in Bangladesh, CARD hoped to establish the same in the Philippines by working with various stakeholders to create the policy environment, institutions, and products required. And in an environment where policy reform is a distant prospect, FSCC leveraged its royal seal of approval and grassroots appeal to broker a workaround that helped informal childcare providers to register with the Thai government, despite its onerous regulations.

Reasons for collaboration vary, as do the models employed and the degree of engagement in each case. But a partnership with government has been forged by nearly all of the 30 SDOs selected for this study. Across the board, these SDOs have deployed common strategies that have helped them to leverage their engagement with government relations to maximum effect.

For certain SDOs, government partnerships present few conflicts. The alignment of objectives between SRAM and the Malaysian government meant that their successes were mutual, making for an easy partnership. But this is a rarity in the social delivery sector, where agendas are often complex and less than perfectly matched. The SDOs most successful in cutting through the red tape were those that embraced it. Knowing that government officials tended to be overworked and beleaguered, SNEHA created an appreciative atmosphere to encourage collaboration between all actors to strengthen the health system.

But partnering with government does not mean co-option. In fact, an independent streak not only helps successful SDOs to avoid mission creep, but also allows them to appear as credible and valuable partners in the eyes of government. Despite the allure of research grants earmarked for specific policy questions, CEEW's prerogative to set its own research agenda is fiercely guarded by Ghosh. In this way, CEEW is able to remain clear-minded on what it sees to be priorities of the day and to play its role casting the spotlight on them.

Mindful of the vagaries of government spending priorities, SDOs such as Eden Welfare Foundation are generating new revenue streams in efforts to become more self-reliant. But even organizations heavily dependent on government grants to deliver services have carved out the space to pursue their own interests. Recognizing a dearth of government resources flowing to palliative care in Hong Kong, HoH used alternative funds to set up an affordable hospice center. Such initiatives demonstrate the importance of maintaining the independence to identify gaps in public sector provision, and innovating to generate new solutions.

While CARD was ultimately dependent on government to facilitate the conditions for microfinance, it was very much the case of an SDO leading the government. Alip took the initiative in conducting research, generating funds, and planting the seeds for his grand vision to provide microfinance services to the rural poor.

Arguably the greatest successes achieved were those in which the SDO showed governments a better model for service delivery. Of the 30 SDOs studied, SWF's community model for elderly care, Magic Bus's mentorship system, New Homeland Foundation's approach to rebuilding disaster-struck communities, and CARD's delivery of microfinance services through the "aunties" of the countryside have all been adapted by government as national models for service delivery.

Such success speaks to the importance of the lesson: SDOs in Asia must work with authorities at some level. The nature and timing of collaboration varies with the country, the mission, and the organization, but the eventual relationship remains fundamental. For some SDOs, government partnerships are necessary even to begin operations, and for many more, they offer greater reach in their ongoing efforts.

Note

1. In China, similar to several other Asian countries, there are GONGOs, which is an acronym for government operated non-governmental organizations. Seemingly oxymoronic in a Western context, it makes complete sense in Asia.

CHAPTER 7

Not Just Giving: How Do Companies Play?

Ruth A. Shapiro

In Asia, many companies have been quietly addressing local problems through a familiar model: that of family patronage. The deep cultural roots of family influence have taken Asian development along a different path than that taken in the United States and Europe, despite certain parallels in their economic growth.

Family influence matters greatly in Asian economies, though not every nation is identical. Some markets have developed within democratic systems and some under authoritarian regimes. Certain governments have erected barriers to foreign investment, while others have embraced international capital. Some countries have advanced economies, with the GDPs of Japan, South Korea, and Singapore among the highest in the world. Some remain poor, while others such as China, India, and Indonesia are an unusual mix, having created vast wealth and a rising middle class, yet retaining a significant populace living on less than $2 per day.

Despite this variation, there are important cultural characteristics shared across the region. One of the most important is the value of families in the overall economic systems.

The notion of a company itself as family forms an intrinsic part of Asian economic life. In this model, the owner/CEO treats workers as extended family, particularly in companies in which the family plays a dominant role.

R.A. Shapiro
CAPS, Hong Kong SAR, China

R.A. Shapiro et al., *Pragmatic Philanthropy*,
https://doi.org/10.1007/978-981-10-7119-5_7

Today, Asian companies typically have more professional employees, yet family remains an important driver of corporate decisions, including how a company relates to its surrounding community.

In fact, according to a 2013 KPMG study, a significant percentage of companies in many Asian countries with market capitalization of more than US$50 million remain family dominated. The chart below shows how prevalent family control is in Asia.

India: 67%
Philippines: 66%
Thailand: 66%
Singapore: 63%
Malaysia: 62%
Indonesia: 61%
Hong Kong: 62%
South Korea: 58%

Japan, China, and to some degree Taiwan, are countries where family-dominant firms are not in the majority, but still even in these countries, there are family-controlled firms that are important mainstays.

For those not as familiar with this phenomenon, it can be difficult to convey how integrated families are in all aspects of business life. I recall once bringing a famous American business guru to meet with a group of Asian business leaders. His talk wasn't going well, and I called for a coffee break to talk to him about changing gears and moving to a new topic. He said he knew exactly what to do and strode off confidently to restart the session. "Let me now address something that everyone cares deeply about," he said. "Work-life balance…"—I cannot begin to explain what a dud that comment was! Work-life balance is not an issue in Asia the way it is in the West. Work is life and one's friends are also one's business partners. Families are involved in business in their daily lives, affecting with whom they dine and, absolutely, whom they trust. This is true when making business decisions, and it is very much the case when making philanthropic decisions. The borders between these different worlds, much more delineated in the West, are often blurred and overlapping in Asia.

Family control is important to understand when looking at a company's corporate social responsibility (CSR) programs and the focus of its philanthropy. It is quite common for a family to route its philanthropy through the company rather than create a separate personal foundation. I have had numerous conversations with ultra-high-net-worth individuals who automatically consider their philanthropy through the company instead of setting up a separate family foundation. The company and the family remain tightly linked in many Asian economies.

A 2011 UBS/Insead report on Asian philanthropy says, "One has to be cognizant of the fact that in Asia it is hard to establish degrees of separation between family philanthropy and company philanthropy/CSR. Often what is seen as individual or family giving is "company giving" now practiced through the establishment of company foundations and trusts."[1]

When a family is in charge, there tend to be certain common practices. First, the philanthropy is very much aligned with the personal interests and connections of the patriarch. This is slowly starting to change as the second and third generations go to foreign business schools and return home with new ideas about CSR, including the notion of impact investing and social enterprise support—topics we will explore in greater depth later in Chapter 8. A second typical practice is to run the company foundation under a member of the family, usually a wife, daughter, or niece. This person represents the family and allows the chairman to have any final say. In Asia, despite divisions by sex in many business practices, it is culturally acceptable to have a female family member lead philanthropic efforts. There are many examples. In India, Nita Ambani, wife of multi-billionaire Mukesh Ambani, runs the Reliance Foundation, the philanthropic arm of the Reliance Corporation. In China, the Wahaha Charitable Foundation is run by Kelly Fuli Zong, daughter of founder and chairman Zong Qinghou. The Lopez Group Foundation in the Philippines is run by 11 family members, with Mercedes Lopez Vargas as the president.

In a company dominated by a family, the patriarch often still plays the critical role. This dual persona of chief executive and father figure will likely remain in place in Asia because it adheres to norms that work within many Asian societies. The fuzzy distinction between family and company reflects the larger context of the fundamental use and appreciation of relationships. As Li and Redding write, "Across the board, Asian economies are rich in interpersonal trust, as expressed in extensive networks of reciprocal relationships between individuals both inside the firm and outside." Asian societies do tend to build stronger interpersonal networks than their Western counterparts, both inside the family and with friends, leveraging them for business.[2] It stands to reason that if personal relationships play a major role in business, they would be at least as important in situations in which there is no clear bottom line, like philanthropy.

Even in countries where the family/corporation lines have become clearer such as Japan and Taiwan, we can see a greater comfort level with the company acting in a patriarchal fashion. In Asia, especially Japan, company towns are thriving. In a company town, the company provides many of the social services such as schools, elder care, sports, and recreational activities, and while the term has become anathema in the West, company towns are thriving in Asia. Positions in towns like Toyota City are eagerly sought. There is a comfort level with the company taking on the role of avuncular benefactor that does not have an equivalent in most Western societies.

Company towns are even increasing in Asia, while they decline in Europe and America. In January 2011, *The Economist* wrote, "What is dying in the West is surviving or being reborn in the emerging world. New company towns are being constructed from nothing ... and old ones are being given a new lease of life."[3]

One of the most notable company towns is Jamshedpur, the home of Tata Steel. Established in the early twentieth century, Tata Steel and its affiliate companies provide housing, health care, schools, utilities, and sporting fields and equipment. In an interview in 2016, Ratan Tata, former chairman of the Tata Group, explained how his appreciation for interconnectivity between the company and its employees was forged during his visits to Jamshedpur early in his tenure with the group.

Understanding the role of companies in Asian philanthropy requires seeing the pivotal role that families still play in Asian companies, the related acceptance of patriarchal tendencies, and also the degree to which interpersonal relationships are cultivated and valued. The notions of family and community are integral to many companies in Asia.

Given the oligarchic nature of many Asian markets, it is easy to appreciate the critical role that companies can play in delivering social goods to their communities. Within the last few years, virtually all companies have become expected to pursue philanthropic activities, and while some are slow to engage in a significant manner, many have embraced their roles as benefactors, with senior managers and family members devoting considerable time to their programs.

Companies employ different approaches when taking on a role in social delivery. This chapter describes eight:

1. *Corporate Philanthropy*
2. *Volunteerism*
3. *Shared Value*
4. *Social Business*
5. *DIY*
6. *Funding a Corporate Need*

7. *Alliances*
8. *Longer-term Partnerships*

Many companies in Asia use several of these strategies at the same time, but they are distinct and each worthy of explanation and illustration. They also have unique applications within Asia. While the strategies described are employed by firms around the world, those in the region have developed them in culturally appropriate ways.

1. *Corporate Philanthropy*

The first and most prevalent technique is direct funding of local nonprofit organizations. Corporate philanthropy has been on the rise for a decade and continues to grow, despite some economic hard times. In 2012, 66 percent of all charitable giving in China came from corporations, according to the Conference Board. India also sees substantial corporate support for CSR, especially after new legislation requiring top companies to direct 2 percent of after-tax income to certified CSR activities. According to finance minister Arun Jaitley in a March 2016 *Economic Times* article, companies spent Rs8347 crore (more than US$1.2 billion) in the previous year.

Our case studies illustrate how much corporate philanthropy means to many SDOs in Asia. Bainian Vocational Services, which offers vocational training to migrant and rural teens, gets 51 percent of its budget from local Chinese and multinational corporations. Mercy Malaysia receives 45 percent of its funding from companies. The Magic Bus in India receives 51 percent of its funding from corporations. (In other chapters, we have discussed how most SDOs in Asia do not have the capacity to keep accurate records, maintain transparency and evaluate impact. In all 30 case studies, we asked for the percentage of overall donations that come from corporations; only five were able to answer the question specifically, although most acknowledged the importance of corporate support to their overall budget.)

With traditional corporate philanthropy, a company supports nonprofit organizations in areas determined by management. In Asia, that is often education, the most popular area for funding across all countries. In any case, the company responds to a proposal or identifies SDOs with which it wants to work. Participation typically involves a simple transfer of funds. Relationships between the company and the SDO may go on for years when designed as a partnership, with the company providing financial resources and the SDO carrying out a program approved by the company.

Western companies tend to work in this fashion as well. They identify a need they want to address and then find the SDO partner that has the capability and experience to deliver that good. For the SDO, corporate support can be a tremendous boon.

Oftentimes, however, the relationship between the two entities encounters difficulties. Companies and SDOs might have different approaches and necessarily have different aims. In a 1999 book *Corporate-NGO Partnership in Asia-Pacific*, editor Tadashi Yamamoto writes of the numerous challenges that face ongoing corporate-NGO partnerships. During our work, we have found two innovative programs that seek to address these challenges and improve the relationships between companies and SDOs. CCPHI is an Indonesian nonprofit that promotes partnerships among companies, NGOs, and local governments to encourage sustainable communities. CCPHI acts as a sort of marriage counselor to the corporate-SDO partners. Every relationship needs a third party from time to time. CCPHI acts as that third party, offering training, counseling, and tools for effective and sustainable corporate–SDO partnerships.

Singapore Management University (SMU) has also developed a program to address the disconnect that often occurs between companies, SDOs, and the government. In the new Master of Tri-Sector Collaboration degree program now offered, students learn skills to traverse the barriers between these three parts of society. Center Director Martin Tan says, "As societal issues in the world become more complex, we need to recognize that there isn't a one-size-fits-all approach to solving these issues nor will there be one single entity that will have all the answers. Not the government, businesses, or civil society on its own. However, we could if we collaborate across all sectors and leverage on each other's strengths and expertise to address some of society's greatest challenges collectively." This course, now in its second year, is the only one of its kind in the world.

Both SMU's program and CCPHI offer innovative means to bring about more effective partnerships. Both recognize that the need to work together to solve complex problems, while still relatively untested in Asia, will be critical going forward.

2. *Volunteerism*

Another tactic embraced by many Asian companies is volunteerism. A popular activity is arranging a specific day when employees are encouraged to clean a park, build a house, or teach a workshop. Many times, employees are encouraged to raise funds themselves, which are matched by the company. While these activities do not bring about systemic change, they do solve a targeted problem and give the employees a sense of pride and shared values with their employer. Li & Fung, based in Hong Kong, provides a good example of such volunteerism, along with other kinds of philanthropy. The Li & Fung team in Pakistan has identified a girls' school that receives financial support from both Li & Fung employees and management. The employees have offered workshops there on hygiene and public speaking to help the girls feel more empowered.

3. *Shared Value*

Companies also engage with the community through shared value initiatives. Shared value, a term coined by Michael Porter and Mark Kramer in 2011, refers to a strategy whereby companies bring economic value to themselves while addressing a social need. In their seminal article introducing this concept, they wrote, "Not all profit is equal.... Profits involving a social purpose represent a higher form of capitalism, one that creates a positive cycle of company and community prosperity."

While there has been much talk and excitement about shared value in Asia, there are few examples of Asian companies successfully carrying it out. One of the more notable cases of this work is Manila Water in the Philippines. Manila Water figured out how to decrease siphoning and protect the pipeline so that clean, cheaper water reached those in the poorest districts of Manila. This successful project improved water access for the poor while at the same time increasing Manila Water's bottom line. Jaime Zobel de Ayala, chairman and CEO of the Ayala Group, the holding company that includes Manila Water, has said, "Meeting social needs should be embedded in our business models and should be undertaken using the same disciplines as those of business."

Another example of shared value is Kirin Beverage Company's Hyoketsu Wanashi pear juice. Kirin developed the product using pears from the Fukushima region as a way to support local farmers after the earthquake and tsunami that devastated that region. In addition to supporting the community, Hyoketsu Wanashi has been a great commercial success.

Not surprisingly, shared value is an appealing concept. Shared value does not entail corporate philanthropy but can solve a social problem and generate profit at the same time, aligning incentives and buttressing programmatic sustainability. When the company and the community prosper, the initiatives are more sustainable over time. At this stage, shared value initiatives are new globally and very new in Asia. We can expect to see much more innovation from work of this kind in the years to come.

4. *Social Business*

In some ways, the opposite approach to shared value is the notion of "social businesses." This term, coined by Nobel Laureate Muhammad Yunus in his 2010 seminal book ***Building Social Business***, designates companies choosing to forego profits in order to conduct a business that brings significant social benefits. Yunus has created several of these in Bangladesh, including one with clothing maker Uniqlo. In this social business, Grameen Uniqlo has established manufacturing plants employing local workers, to create a less-expensive line of clothing sold locally, at cost. In collaboration with Yunus and the Grameen Foundation, several companies have created social businesses in Bangladesh, including Veolia Water, Danone, and Intel.

Though these are wonderful initiatives, it is not clear that large companies would choose to forego profits if not for the involvement of an acclaimed Nobel prize winner. Partnering with Mohammad Yunus entails additional benefits for multinational companies as they garner high-profile approval from the public. Some companies in Asia have taken a different approach by creating social enterprises that, unlike social businesses, are independent of the larger firm. These will be discussed in greater detail in Chapter 8.

5. *DIY*

The fourth strategy for community engagement is direct delivery of a social good, when companies arrange to do the work on their own. Those that do this believe, often with some justification, that they have the skills to deliver a social good more efficiently than by working through an NGO.

SM Holdings in the Philippines did just this with its BDO Foundation for building clinics and schools in the typhoon–ravaged areas of Leyte and Samar. The Federation of Filipino Chinese Chamber of Commerce and Industry Inc. followed a similar route, building 6000 schools throughout the Philippines. The Reliance Foundation also develops its own intervention strategies and carries out work through its own initiatives in rural development, health, and education.

In China, Lenovo has put in place the Lenovo Youth Public Entrepreneurship program, a company effort to transfer skills from Lenovo employees to start-up social entrepreneurs. Lenovo employees help provide training, venture capital, and instruction in public speaking and other skills so that young college students interested in careers in public entrepreneurship can have a greater chance of success.

6. *Funding a Corporate Need*

A fifth, related strategy is to offer services that companies themselves need. This is primarily done in education and training. Many companies find that they cannot find the talent they require, so they have created training programs to promote the necessary skills in current and future employees.

Skill training is not limited to Asian companies, of course. It takes place globally, and in emerging economies around the world, it is often a fundamental part of employment. It can be helpful to the employee and the company, but it does not address the larger societal problems of poor schools and an unprepared workforce. In interviews, a number of executives expressed interest in developing more comprehensive schemes to create win-win-win outcomes: employee, company, and society at large.

7. *Alliances*

In some cases, corporations and corporate leaders find it useful to develop an alliance or consortium to bring about change. Recognizing that the Philippines needed coordinated responses to typhoons, Jaime Zobel de Ayala of the Ayala Group and Manny Pangilinan of PLDT created the Philippine Disaster Recovery Foundation, which is building a disaster operations center to manage private sector efforts for relief. In China, corporate leaders have come together to create the SEE Foundation to address environmental issues and the Ai You Foundation to provide medical aid to children. In Malaysia, under the leadership of Yayasan Hasanah, the philanthropic arm of the nation's sovereign wealth fund, the Yayasan Amir program finds corporate sponsors for schools that have adopted the Yayasan Hasanah curriculum. Alliances like these can leverage and coordinate resources and donations in ways that do-it-alone strategies cannot.

8. *Longer-term Partnerships*

The last way to engage is the one that we believe has the greatest potential in Asia, a hybrid of the outreach strategies described earlier. Many companies blend a variety of skills with a longer term, venture capital approach. They place the skills that make companies successful alongside financial resources to build the capacity of SDO partners to bring about sustainable change.

SDOs may be nonprofits, but they need to think more like businesses. To maximize their impact, they should be concerned with transparent accounting, financial forecasting, strategic planning, organizational management and development, and a whole host of other skills that have traditionally been labeled as business skills. These skills are in ample supply within the private sector.

While illustrative examples of this type of partnership are not yet in great supply, there are some pointing the way forward. Here are three examples in India, Malaysia, and Thailand.

Dilasa Sanstha has been working with farming communities in India for 20 years, with the goal of increasing production and stabilizing livelihoods. Several years ago, Dilasa entered into a strategic partnership with the Axis Bank Foundation. ABF helped Dilasa set up funding to expand rural credit. It also assisted Dilasa with its internal budgeting and accounting system, and it supported the creation of a monitoring and evaluation system. With ABF's help, for the first time, Dilasa could collect critical impact data on beneficiary income, household assets, migration level, education levels, diet, investment plans, and insurance policies. The partnership with ABF enabled Dilasa to operate at a much larger scale and to help a great many more farmers and rural communities.

Another example of this kind comes from Malaysia. Mercy Malaysia began with a small group of doctors who wanted to provide relief from natural disasters. But they found it difficult to create the systems necessary for nimble and effective response to unforeseen events, so they partnered with Khazanah Berhad, the sovereign wealth fund. Khazanah helped Mercy develop management systems to efficiently deploy people and resources to a disaster zone. The partnership has helped Mercy become a serious and internationally acclaimed provider of disaster assistance around the world. Dato Sri Azman Mokhtar, CEO of Khazanah, said that its work will help broaden Mercy Malaysia's impact by strengthening its service delivery, governance, and financial sustainability.

In Thailand, Siam Commercial Bank has partnered with the Songkhla Forum, a nonprofit organization based in the southern Songkhla province. In 2012, Siam Commercial Bank revamped its CSR program and decided to focus its attention on youth-related services. It also decided that rather than just providing financial support, it would enter into a longer-term partnership with a youth-related SDO to help it became more strategic, better managed, and better governed. Songkhla Forum, with its services for at-risk youth, was a natural match. In addition to management support and financial assistance, the bank has provided help with finance and accounting, HR management, data management, and strategic development.

In all of these three cases, the companies provided financial resources *and* technical resources. They committed to the SDOs for the longer term, developing the trust and the relationships necessary to make the partnerships really work. These models point the way to an exciting new trend, of the deployment of business skills for social good.

Although the strategies may differ, the change in corporate attitude is clear. Moved by consistent public expectations for doing good, companies realize they must engage with their communities; the only question is how. Throughout the region, Asian firms are on the front lines of creating innovative community engagement strategies, to be long-term stakeholders in the region's continued growth. Companies designed on the long-standing family model often find this a natural transition.

Asian companies are not the only ones testing the boundaries of company involvement; exciting new trends and innovation are taking place around the world. What is true in Asia, however, is that much of the innovation stems from long-held values and practices. Families remain important, and the role of the family in company decision-making is critical. As we saw in the do-it-yourself strategies of Reliance and SM Holdings, in Li & Fung's community outreach, and with the Wahaha company foundation in China, family-led CSR programs are not only the norm but exemplify company-community engagement. Families desire to be around for the long term. They have the control to look beyond quarterly reporting and to take a longer-term view that creates value for them and the communities in which they operate.

Notes

1. UBS INSEAD Study on Family Philanthropy. p. 23. http://sites.insead.edu/social_entrepreneurship/documents/insead_study_family_philantropy_asia.pdf. Accessed August 20, 2014.
2. Li, Peter Ping and Gordon Redding. "Social Capital in Asia: Its Dual Nature and Function." In *The Oxford Handbook of Asian Business Systems*. Ed. Michael Witt and Gordon Redding. Oxford University Press, Oxford, UK, 2014, pp. 313–333.
3. https://www.economist.com/blogs/schumpeter/2011/01/company_towns. Accessed January 11, 2017.

CHAPTER 8

Impact Investing in Asia: Just Getting Started

Ruth A. Shapiro

For most of the twentieth century, nonprofit organizations relied on a static funding model: foundations supplied grants to charities that delivered services otherwise not available for a variety of reasons, including budgetary constraints (for example, health care for the poor) or because of the innovative but still unproven nature of the work (for example, new models of helping at-risk youth).

Beginning in the early 1980s, nonprofit organizations evolved and diversified, taking on new characteristics throughout the 1990s that would change the way philanthropists and nonprofit organizations now think about and act on their work. Many of these changes result from an increased understanding and application of the tenets of social entrepreneurship.

In 1981, Bill Drayton introduced the concept of a social entrepreneur when he created Ashoka, now a global leader in incubating talent and ideas in the social sector. Drayton put forward the idea that a social entrepreneur is someone who takes the passion and rigor of an entrepreneur and applies it to a social problem. This was a new idea in two important ways. First, most philanthropy up until that point focused on the organization rather than on its leadership and talent. Second, it introduced the notion that nonprofits should still follow basic business tenets, including sound management, transparent accounting, and strategic planning.

R.A. Shapiro
CAPS, Hong Kong SAR, China

R.A. Shapiro et al., *Pragmatic Philanthropy*,
https://doi.org/10.1007/978-981-10-7119-5_8

Since that time, these ideas have led to a host of changes and innovations that have changed the sector in important ways.

The first major change has been the blurring of the previously sacrosanct demarcation between profit and nonprofit. What started off as the adoption of corporate rigor has evolved into the implementation of numerous business tools, such as the use of profit as a motive or the notion that key performance indicators (KPIs) are applicable in nonprofit management as well. This has shaken out with organizations sitting at various points on the profit–nonprofit continuum, offering an array of options for funders.

One of the most powerful social investment trends to emerge from this new thinking is the creation of social enterprises on the organizational side and impact investing on the funding side. The term *social enterprise* is used often to refer to a host of initiatives and models. A social enterprise must perform the delicate balancing act of meeting its financial obligations while staying true to its social imperatives.

Impact Investing and Asia

On the funding side, charitable application of the profit motive is called "impact investing." The Global Impact Investing Network (GIIN) defines impact investments as "investments made into companies, organizations, and funds with the intention to generate social and environmental impact alongside financial returns." Once again, there is variation, but mostly in terms of expectations of what kinds of financial returns the investor is looking to receive. The Acumen Fund, a pioneer impact investment fund, uses the term *patient capital* to indicate a time lag before seeing returns for the companies in its portfolio, perhaps at below-market rates. In Asia, Acumen has invested $31.9 million spread over 26 companies in India, and in Pakistan, $15 million in 16 companies. Their funds promote affordable housing, solar power, and private education, among other things.

Private equity giant TPG's new social development fund, Rise, sits on the side of the return spectrum offering market returns for its investors. In addition to big names such as Bono and Jeff Skoll, Rise has attracted several pension and sovereign wealth funds. *The New York Times* reports that three such funds have invested nine-figure sums. In the same article, Rise managing partner Bill McGlashan says, "The reality is that no matter which side of the aisle you're on, and no matter where your framework is, if I can build a great business that's profitable and successful and, oh, by the way, here's the impact and the multiple of impact that's created through that business's successes, I think that's good for everybody."[1] Rise targets businesses that are building infrastructure, telecom, energy, and for-profit education.[2]

Even the Ford Foundation has joined in. In March 2017, Darren Walker, the foundation's president, announced that it would commit $1 billion to investments that "earn not only attractive financial returns but concrete social returns as well."[3]

While the Acumen Fund and TPG are on different sides of the profitability spectrum, they are both committed to finding meaningful measurements of impact, specifically how much these companies contribute to solving a problem in addition to bringing in financial returns. In 2016, GIIN released its sixth Annual Impact Investor Survey. It reports that of the 158 respondents to the survey, 60 percent principally target risk-adjusted, market-rate returns, while 25 percent target "below market-rate returns: closer to market rate" and 16 percent target "below market-rate returns: closer to capital preservation."[4]

But Asia remains far from the center of the impact-investing sector. According to this survey, which includes most of the established fund managers in the field, only 5 percent of assets under management are in East and Southeast Asia and 8 percent in South Asia. Very little of that investment occurs in Asia, especially outside of India and Pakistan, a finding consistent with our research. While some of Asia shares in the growing interest and buzz around impact investing, it sees little such activity taking place on the ground. There are several reasons for this.

First is the availability of deals—or more accurately the lack thereof. Though there is desire on the part of social entrepreneurs and investors, there aren't as many social enterprises offering viable business plans. In fact, LGT Venture Philanthropy, one of the larger and most active funds, selected only 25 companies to pursue, of the 5000 considered.[5] Six are now active in the LGT venture portfolio.

On the funding side, investors in Asia have not embraced impact investing to the extent that is taking place on other continents. In a recent *South China Morning Post* article, Stephen Tong, an investment consultant at global professional services firm Willis Towers Watson, said, "In Asia, many asset managers still see sustainable investment only as a risk-control tool to exclude certain sectors such as tobacco, rather than adopting a proactive and broader approach to build a portfolio with their own sustainable criteria."[6] In the same article, Annie Chen, who might be the most informed impact investor in Asia, said that despite Hong Kong's role as a global financial center, the city lagged in the development of sustainable

Table 8.1 Partial List of Impact Investing Funds in Asia

China	NPI (Non-profit Incubator), You Change (China Social Entrepreneur Foundation)
Hong Kong	SOW Asia, Social Ventures Hong Kong, The Good Lab, Synergy Social Ventures
India	Dasra, Start Up!, UnLtd India, Deshpande Fund, Villgro, Khosla Labs
Indonesia	UnLtd Indonesia, Platform Usaha Sosial
Japan	Japan Venture Philanthropy Fund, Entrepreneurial Training for Innovative Communities (ETIC)
Malaysia	Social Enterprise Malaysia, My Harapan, Yayasan Hasanah
Philippines	ChooseSocial.PH, Philippine Social Enterprise Network, Institute for Social Entrepreneurship in Asia, PRESENT Coalition
Singapore	Singapore Centre for Social Enterprise (raiSE), Social Innovation Park, Social Enterprise Association
South Korea	Innov8social, Social Enterprise Leaders Forum (SELF), Work Together Foundation, SK Happiness Foundation
Taiwan	Social Enterprise Insights, Social Enterprise Development Association
Thailand	ChangeFusion, C asean

Source: Compiled by the Centre for Asian Philanthropy and Society (CAPS) 2016–2017

investment, lacking both demand and supply of such expertise compared to other global financial cities.[7]

Asia's lack of deals and interest in impact investing are changing, however. There is a great deal of enthusiasm around the subject. One indicator of this interest has been the increase in the number of conferences in Asia devoted to social enterprises and impact investing. These have included the International Symposium of Social Entrepreneurship (ISSE) 2016 (Singapore), Asian Venture Philanthropy Network (Hong Kong), Dasra Philanthropy Forum (India), Social Enterprise Summit (Hong Kong), and the Korea Impact Investing Network (South Korea), among others.

Another important trend in Asia is the increase in the number of local funds that provide financial and management assistance to start-up social enterprises. A partial list is shown in Table 8.1.

Governments Join In

In addition to nonprofit initiatives, many governments in Asia are getting into the game. Hong Kong, Singapore, Thailand, South Korea, India, Malaysia, Taiwan, and Indonesia have each established funds to support the creation of social enterprises. The tricky part here is the definition of a social enterprise and the role the government can provide in supporting their creation and viability. There is great variability across countries.

The India Fund highlights the goal of supporting world-class enterprises that focus on the problems of the poor, a broad category. South Korea identifies such an organization as "a company that performs business activities while putting priority on the pursuit of social purposes." This definition stresses the primacy of the social bottom line. A social enterprise has to meet its financial obligations while also remaining committed to its social imperatives.

The challenge of this balancing act was made terribly clear by the case of SKS Financial, in the Indian state of Andhra Pradesh. Unable to pursue both goals simultaneously, SKS veered toward profit first, resulting in the state government closing it down after numerous suicides by overleveraged borrowers.

And it is not alone. Mohammed Yunus of Grameen Bank warned at the time of its IPO that by going public, there would be incredible market pressure to focus on financial returns. In response to such concerns, the Benefit Corporation or B Corp accreditation system was created in the United States and is now operating globally. Once accredited as a B Corporation, a company must maintain strict compliance with the profitability/purpose goals of the company. The first Indian company to become a certified B Corporation is eKutir, which listed in June, 2016. In China and Japan, three social enterprises are now listed. South Korea has the most, with ten social enterprises listed. It is fair to say this statistic shows that enthusiasm for social enterprises runs high in South Korea.

The most important component of government schemes is the availability of capital, especially in the start-up phase of the effort. Again, there is great variability. Singapore has put US$6 million into two funds for social enterprises; one for grants and the other for impact investment. South Korea has put US$28.3 million in its social enterprise support fund, and Thailand provides $1.2 million in financial resources to social enterprises. For India, according to the *Business Standard* at the time of the announcement, the India Fund was seeded with Rs500 crore (about US$77.5 million)[8] and expects to expand to Rs5000 crore once launched.

All of these funds also offer ancillary types of support such as help with networking, mentoring, incubation hubs, and registration assistance. The key question here is who is doing the mentoring? Generally, government bureaucrats and officials do not necessary know what makes a business plan viable. It is important that people with on-the-ground business experience come into the mix and apply their experience to the projects. In Hong Kong, the Social Enterprise Partnership Programme does so by serving as matchmaker between start-up social enterprises and private sector mentors who work with the teams as they develop their ideas and launch them as businesses.

Social Enterprises

During our project, we included two types of social enterprises among our case studies—those that are businesses with a dual bottom line; and those that are hybrids, organizations that include profitable and not-for-profit components.

There were three social enterprises in our study that adhered to the South Korean definition; namely, businesses primarily promoting a social bottom line. Tree Planet is one such South Korean company and a registered B Corporation. Tree Planet leverages online entertainment to carry out conservation projects in two ways. It began by incorporating payment for tree planting into mobile gaming applications and web games. In these games, a player can choose to nurture a tree by paying a small fee, which is then used by the Tree Planet team to plant trees in South Korea and in ten other countries.

After working with the gaming app for some time, the Tree Planet managers realized that there was another way to encourage young people to support tree planting. They conceived of the idea of "star forests." Star forests capitalize on the extraordinary popularity throughout Asia of "K-Pop" or Korean music and drama stars. Fans pay for the planting of trees associated with their favorite star. In both the gaming and star forest initiatives, the government provides the land at no cost to Tree Planet. According to Tree Planet's website, it has planted 509,568 trees since its inception.

Landwasher, based in China, makes similar use of government partnership, but it did not begin that way. In 1999, Hao Wu left his job with a securities firm to address the need for sanitation in a country facing severe water shortages. He developed a waterless toilet with the intent of making it available throughout China but most especially in arid, rural areas. Landwasher was making some progress in building its business in rural China, but growth was somewhat slow due to the rather steep price tag of $5000 to $8000 for a 4-unit toilet system. Then in 2008 it received a huge deal from the Beijing municipal government to supply all the toilets set up during the Beijing summer Olympics. According to Landwasher, it saved an estimated 1000 metric tons of water during the two weeks of the Olympic Games.[9] Since that time, Landwasher has been the "go-to" source of sanitation systems for large, government-organized events in China. Now that Landwasher has become a successful business, it is turning back to its original purpose of providing sanitation systems to poor, rural areas. It is working on developing a lower-priced model. According to founder Wu, this is the most important challenge it faces today.[10]

Indonesia's Telapak, the third social enterprise included in our study, also began with modest roots. Its two founders, Ambrosius Ruwindrijarto and Silverius Oscar Unggul, started off as investigative journalists. They began working together on Telapak when they founded a radio station that informed local citizens about illegal logging taking place in their communities.

Since then, Telapak has branched into sustainable community logging, and it also advises companies on sustainability and CSR activities in Indonesia. It has become an association of multiple stakeholders committed to environmental conservation and protection. They work together to provide assistance to farmers, nonprofit groups working on environmental issues, businesses, and the government. Telapak has created a unique system that allows it to call upon relevant skill sets of those within the association to address a particular challenge, responding to numerous requests from companies and aid agencies in the past several years. It has proved a winning model, earning the organization and its leadership the prestigious Ramon Magsaysay Foundation Award, the Skoll Social Entrepreneur Award, and an Ashoka Fellowship.

All three of these case studies share several important elements. First, of course, they were founded by passionate and driven social entrepreneurs committed to a cleaner, more sustainable community and world. Second, they evolved in ways that used different strategies than originally planned, while maintaining the essential mission of the work. When harnessing market forces to succeed, a business must follow the market drivers. In the cases cited above, the path took the companies in new directions. Tree Planet realized that building star forests leveraged the almost cult status enjoyed by Korean K-Pop celebrities. Landwasher and Telapak became much more commercial. By selling sanitation systems to the Chinese government, Landwasher provided a much-needed public good, albeit not in the countryside where Hao Wu first made his decision to create an innovative social enterprise. Telapak must grapple with the balance of assisting local and multinational corporations as a consultant, while also criticizing them for activities causing environmental degradation.

Each of the organizations also tackles the challenge of assessment. Balancing profit and mission is always a challenge for social enterprises. Ideally, most can tackle this challenge when first designing their business plans. Once beyond that, however, the balancing act continues. All three of these social enterprises, like many others in the field, must also contend with the twin challenges of measurement versus mission.

As noted at the beginning of this chapter, businesses that try to "do good and do well" create a laudable but challenging goal for themselves. It does take discipline and commitment to maintain that delicate balance, a task that can be made easier when progress toward each goal can be measured. With that in mind, the Western world has put serious effort into finding measurement systems that capture the impact of an enterprise in addition to its sustainability. Rise, the TPG fund, has partnered with Bridgespan to create a "rigorous set of metrics with which to measure performance."[11] In announcing the Ford Foundation's commitment to provide US$1 billion to mission-related investments over the next ten years, the foundation stated that impact assessments have evolved sufficiently to warrant this type of investment.[12]

Asian organizations followed. The models from the West aren't ideal; they see mixed success, as it is difficult to develop frameworks on intangible benefits that can accrue. But some social enterprises' goods and services lend themselves more readily to impact assessment. Landwasher measures its success on how many toilets were set up and the tonnage of water that was saved by using its systems. Tree Planet measures how many trees and how many forests were planted as a result of its work. Educate Girls, a social enterprise offering fee-based educational opportunities for girls in Rajasthan, India, can measure the number of girls who received an education through its programs. All of these offer a product or service that had not been available previously. Their work, by definition, represents a net gain of services to the community.

Measurement becomes trickier when there are confounding variables. For example, while Telapak can say that during the time it has been involved in a community, illegal logging decreased, it cannot claim clear causality. Telapak itself does not feel comfortable taking this credit. "We don't want to be arrogant by telling people how much impact we have created to the community," said Khusnul Zaini, Telapak's president.[13]

In such cases, some organizations employ impact analyses that adhere to local situations. For example, to buttress arguments in favor of microfinance, the Grameen Foundation created the Progress out of Poverty Index (PPI). Aris Alip of the Center for Agriculture and Rural Development (CARD) says of PPI, "Now we have objective poverty data on our clients thanks to the Progress out of Poverty Index and Grameen Foundation's guidance on analysis; the results challenge us to do better."[14] The challenge with the PPI is that it measures changes in poverty, but cannot show causality with the loans that the borrowers received.

Another similarity between the social enterprises in our study is the extraordinary degree of international acclaim and attention they have garnered. Telapak's awards are listed above. Tree Planet has received the Reddot Design Award, Google Innovation Award, and the iF design award, among others. Landwasher was picked by *Fast Company* as one of the 50 most innovative companies in 2013.

That isn't by accident. We wanted to study successful social delivery organizations (SDOs), and since international acclaim is one indicator of success, it's only natural that our case studies found firms garnering accolades. But there is more to it than that. Because there are few successful social enterprises in Asia, those that do succeed reap a great deal of attention and kudos. These high-performing organizations ride the wave of interest in impact investing amid a scarcity of alternatives, especially in East and Southeast Asia.

Lastly, all three social enterprises in our study benefit from a larger phenomenon of excitement about social enterprises, especially among young people. The Royal Bank of Scotland conducted a study that showed that people between the ages of 18–30 were more likely than the general population to want to start up a social enterprise (27 percent, compared to 20 percent), and more likely to consider supporting social causes that they are passionate about (70 percent, compared to 63 percent of the general population).[15] Although no one tracks the actual ages of those running social enterprises in Asia, there is a great deal of anecdotal evidence favoring the young. Nini Daing, CEO of MyHarapan, a youth-focused organization in Malaysia, puts it best: "The challenges we face today require the naivety of our youth, our rebels with a cause, who are redefining success in their pursuit of a more meaningful life. The good news is that young people today are doing just this by rising up to take on these complex challenges to an unprecedented degree."[16]

Hybrid Projects

There is one other type of social enterprise that is becoming more common in Asia: a hybrid organization. Here, that means a nonprofit organization that pursues social good while also supporting a business model that may work with its mandate, thereby creating sustainable income streams. In our case studies, there are three examples of this: Eden Social Welfare Foundation in Taiwan, CARD in the Philippines, and BAIF Development Research Foundation in India.

Eden Social Welfare Foundation was founded by Liu Hsia, herself disabled, to train other disabled people in Taiwan with skills that help them to be productive members of society. This helps them gain self-confidence from their ability to earn an income and contribute to their families' well-being. In the past 30 years, Eden has grown from a staff of two, including Liu Hsia, to an organization that employs 2800 full-time staff across 85 offices in 21 counties and cities. Its budget/funding is now US$49.5 million per annum.[17]

The growth has been extraordinary. Originally focusing on job skills, its services have expanded to include psychological counseling, sheltered workshops, employment referral, talent and skill training, cultural and recreational activities, and gospel delivery. As Eden grew and trained more and more people, they outstripped the jobs available to them, so it began to create its own businesses to employ those it had trained. It started with a small factory employing six people making good quality local handicrafts. Then it expanded into restaurants and bakeries, and then computer training and coding. Now, alongside skill and job training, Eden works with its clients to help with interpersonal and communication training, counseling, and career advice. The businesses that Eden runs are an integral part of its core mission to help disabled people, but they also provide a very real benefit to Eden itself. Last year, 14.4 percent of the total budget came from the businesses it has created. Eden has truly created a win-win situation by building social enterprises alongside its nonprofit programs.

CARD in the Philippines is another great success story. In 1986, Aris Alip and 14 other social entrepreneurs set up a microfinance organization with the goal of providing credit to rural poor involved primarily with agribusiness efforts. Unfortunately, the early results were not promising. Many borrowers did not pay back the loans. So Alip and his colleagues searched for alternative models. One such model was Grameen Bank in

Bangladesh. CARD adapted for the Philippines the women-focused group-lending model that Grameen had pioneered. It included the notion that CARD's customers should also become part of the management of the organization. This way, the reasoning went, CARD would always be customer-focused.

The changes that it put in place made all the difference. CARD now has 30 affiliated organizations and businesses. It owns banks to cater to those customers who have moved beyond micro-credit and need more capital. It offers insurance and education. It has training affiliates for its customers as well as for its own employees. It offers customers and employees low-cost medications. CARD has become a holding company, with some of its portfolio organizations maintaining their nonprofit status while others are social enterprises. They work together, complementing each other and providing a range of services to their customers, many of whom are involved with some aspect of the management of the organization. Through experimentation, a willingness to take risks, staying very close to the needs of rural women, and through the novel combination of nonprofit and social enterprise models, CARD has grown into one of the Philippines' most important SDOs.

A third example of a hybrid organization in our study is BAIF, which works with farmers in India to help them use technology and advanced agribusiness methods to improve their productivity and increase their incomes. Established in 1967, it has helped 5,892,045 families with improved animal husbandry techniques and 201,144 rural families in planting "wadi" orchards, allowing farmers to rear fruit trees, flowers, and vegetables more efficiently.

Inspired by Mahatma Gandhi's call for Indian self-sufficiency, BAIF's founder Manibhai Desai committed himself to improving rural livelihoods. His first important breakthrough was the realization that the milk yields of native Indian Gir cattle went up dramatically when the cows were interbred with Dutch Holstein-Friesian and British Jersey cows. He developed a system for widespread application of artificial insemination that is now being used in 16 Indian states. From the very beginning, BAIF both worked across and brought together its mission-driven ethos with government support, business acumen, and financial reward into a package that creates win-win-win impact. In its multifaceted agribusiness programs, BAIF does seek government and aid agency support, but it also provides numerous jobs to BAIF agricultural technicians and charges farmers for their services. These charges add a crucial income stream to BAIF's bottom line and align commitment between all stakeholders.

In the cases of BAIF, CARD, and Eden, the profitable and the nonprofit, the mission and the enterprise are mutually reinforcing. The business imperative was created as a means to accomplish the humanitarian goals of the organization. In all three cases, the business initiatives grew organically from the needs and opportunities created by the organizations while following their missions. The benefit of this model is that the business angle did not come first, only to be later structured to support the mission. There is less concern with the delicate balance described earlier for social enterprises created as businesses. Of course, not all nonprofit organizations and agendas lend themselves to the creation of social enterprises like BAIF, CARD, and Eden have done, but it is a compelling model and one worth emulating when the circumstances are right.

Conclusion

Enthusiasm for applying business tools and entrepreneurial rigor to social challenges is high, and in many respects getting higher. This trend brings much benefit, along with at least one potential pitfall. On the positive side, there is great energy, talent, and excitement in this space. *Forbes* magazine puts out an annual "Social Entrepreneurs under 30" issue.

If there is any downside to bringing business acumen to the nonprofit world, it may be in excessive expectations. The tag line to that *Forbes* article is "Leveraging business tools to save the world." In the text, *Forbes* says that these young social entrepreneurs are solving the world's toughest problems. This type of language, while extolling the virtues of these endeavors and helping to expand the buzz and excitement around this type of work, also showcases one of the misnomers of the field. Do social enterprises really solve some of the world's greatest challenges?

Taking a look at the three cases in our study, it is difficult to make the argument that any of these social enterprises will solve problems at their root. While Tree Planet does in fact plant trees, it is not solving the widespread problem of deforestation. While Landwasher provides toilets, it is not addressing the need for sanitation systems in arid communities; and while Telapak can advise businesses on how to source commodities in the most sustainable ways possible, it cannot change the way globalization and resource extraction are taking place throughout the world today. Social enterprises do make a positive difference, but we need to be clear that they cannot, in and of themselves, "solve" the biggest challenges. Many of these problems are complex and multifaceted, requiring complex and multifaceted solutions. To really solve these challenges at their most fundamental levels, we need to bring together business and government and civil society in an unprecedented manner.

In Asia, it is critical for donors and policymakers to understand that while promoting social entrepreneurship is great, these efforts cannot be in lieu of other interventions. Rather, they shine as part of a set of initiatives that can work together to address seemingly intractable problems.

Notes

1. *The New York Times*. Dealbook. December 20, 2016. https://www.nytimes.com/2016/12/19/business/dealbook/a-new-fund-seeks-both-financial-and-social-returns.html?_r=0. Accessed December 20, 2016.
2. The Rise Fund corporate website. http://therisefund.com. Accessed February 20, 2017.
3. Ford Foundation News Release. "Ford Foundation Commits $1 Billion from Endowment to Mission Related Investments." April 5, 2017. https://www.fordfoundation.org/the-latest/news/ford-foundation-commits-1-billion-from-endowment-to-mission-related-investments/. Accessed February 20, 2017.
4. Mudaliar, Abhilash, Hannah Schiff and Rachel Bass. "Annual Investor Survey 2016." Global Impact Investing Network, May 2016, p. 12.
5. LGT Venture Philanthropy. "Portfolio Overview." http://www.lgtvp.com/lgt/files/28/28d60948-3cdc-4dd2-85d7-337234845b2f.pdf. Accessed December 10, 2016.
6. South China Morning Post. "Wealth Can Be Green." January 9, 2017.
7. Ibid.
8. Approximately US$77.5 million in May, 2017 exchange rates.
9. Zhang, Tao, Tim Yin, and Christine Yip. "Landwasher, Guardian of the Blue Earth." CAPS Case Study, p. 4.
10. Ibid., p. 7.
11. Sorkin, Andrew Ross. "A New Fund Seeks Both Financial and Social Returns." *The New York Times*, December 20, 2016, p. B1.
12. Ford Foundation News Release. "Ford Foundation Commits $1 Billion from Endowment to Mission Related Investments." April 5, 2017. https://www.fordfoundation.org/the-latest/news/ford-foundation-commits-1-billion-from-endowment-to-mission-related-investments/. Accessed April 20, 2017.
13. Radyati, Maria. "Telapak: Seeking Natural Resource Justice for Communities." CAPS Case Study, p. 10.
14. Progress out of Poverty Index. http://www.progressoutofpoverty.org/testimonials. Accessed April 4, 2017.

15. RBS Enterprise Tracker (in collaboration with Unltd), 2nd quarter, 2013, London, p. 4.
16. In conversation, April 19, 2017.
17. Huang, Ping-Der and Sylph Yang. "Sustainability Through Innovation." CAPS Case Study, p. 2.

CHAPTER 9

A New Social Contract

Ruth A. Shapiro

For those of us working and living in Asia, we have witnessed breathtaking change over the past 30 years. New York City has developed since 1987, too, but nothing compared to the dramatic change in Shanghai or Singapore during the same time period. Easiest to see are the new roads, airports, trains and the buildings, especially the buildings. In 1996, according to the mayor, one in five active construction cranes in the world were in Shanghai. But people are also changing. Asians are part of a global marketplace and cultural community like never before, particularly those in big cities. Connectivity has leapt forward at a blazing pace. From 2015 to 2016 alone, the number of active Internet users jumped 12 percent, and the figure for those with smart phones went up by 21 percent in Asia.[1] There are also extraordinary improvements in education, life expectancy, and other quality of life indicators.

The news, however, is not all good. The Gini coefficient, a measure of the gap between the rich and the poor, is growing around the world. In Asia, this is happening at an accelerated pace. In many respects China is the first superpower to still be a developing country. While one can marvel at the modernity of Asia's cities, there remains great poverty in both urban and rural areas. The dichotomy—between rich and poor, urban and rural, those plugged into the global economy and those very much left out—is glaringly obvious when travelling around many parts of Asia. Some coun-

R.A. Shapiro
CAPS, Hong Kong SAR, China

R.A. Shapiro et al., *Pragmatic Philanthropy*,
https://doi.org/10.1007/978-981-10-7119-5_9

tries have moved into first-world status, including South Korea, Japan, Taiwan, and Singapore, but for the others, the need to deal with a bifurcated set of needs remains a significant challenge.

We have explored in these pages how governments, philanthropists, and nonprofit leaders endeavor to cope with rapid change. The chapter on legal and regulatory reform showcases the various attempts by governments throughout the region to react to new challenges. In fact, much of the legal reform is reactive and thus will undoubtedly bring new and unforeseen problems in the attempts to deal with current problems. The state of regulatory flux will continue as policies are drawn up and tested.

While the economic development of Asia has sped along, many aspects of work and play retain traditional qualities. Throughout this book, we have emphasized the importance of relationships in philanthropic decision-making, social delivery organization (SDO) success, and in the partnerships that often form to address a challenge. However much we hear that relationships matter in Asia, it is a deep truth in the field of charitable work, as the book aims to illustrate. Those who truly succeed in Asia—whether they are in government, in business, or running an SDO—have created, nurtured, and utilized networks and a whole web of relationships.

In our chapter on relationships, we detail the importance they play in the trajectory of an SDO. Relationships bring credibility to CARD in the Philippines. They bring the potential to raise funds for the China Medical Foundation in Hong Kong. They bring expertise to Mercy Malaysia, and they bring the second and third circles of networks for many organizations. Though this is also the case elsewhere in the world, relationships take on much greater significance in environments where skills are in short supply.

For philanthropists, relationships are often the only means by which one can conduct due diligence. The existence of the trust deficit in Asia means that organizations may be viewed with suspicion until proven otherwise, and the involvement of a friend or business partner in an organization provides assurance of credibility and reliability.

Projects championed by government officials gain further currency for donors interested in enhancing *guanxi*, or beneficial relationships. In fact, when I mention that the return on investment for philanthropy is increased *guanxi* to donors, their reaction is most often confirmation. This is not always the case when making philanthropic decisions, but it is certainly prevalent.

As noted in Chapter 2, there is a long history of charitable giving in Asia, but for the most part, the systems that come from organized philanthropy are nascent. In that context, relationships are how one gets something done. It means enlisting the support of someone who can help to accomplish a particular task for a project. We found an example in the mere collection of data for our recent study on enabling environments for philanthropy. Personal networks were essential in getting people to fill out our surveys. Our contacts reached out to theirs and developed *guanxi* as result, strengthening their ties with us and with those they contacted. Both sides appreciated their input, and their roles as interlocutors reinforced the value of their relationships.

While relationships have long been useful, technology is providing new ways of getting things done. Asia has embraced technology along with development. Nine of the top 20 most connected countries in the world are in Asia.[2] Technology has a profound impact on many aspects of social and economic development in the region. In the charitable sector, it changes approaches to business in four important ways: through fundraising, transparency, accountability, and impact.

Crowdfunding is a phenomenon around the world, and in a region as connected as Asia it is becoming a powerful tool. One of the most cited examples is the story of Deng Fei in China and the free lunch program he started. Concerned about hungry kids, Deng Fei asked for support online in 2011 to provide school lunches to kids in poor areas. Within a month, his posting on Weibo (China's Twitter equivalent) generated more than RMB1 million (US$150,000) in small amounts from numerous donors. By the end of 2016, 80,000 children received lunch daily and the government picked up the program to expand it in five provinces.

Technology also enables greater transparency and accountability in two important ways. First, in many Asian countries, online listings include organizations adhering to stricter reporting standards. The Hong Kong Council for Social Services' WiseGiving platform, for example, allows potential donors to find out a great deal of information about the 450 SDOs on their site. The Philippine Council for NGO Certification lists all those certified on its website. There are other such sites in India, Japan, South Korea and China.

The second way that technology makes a difference is as an important watchdog tool. While governments might not have the wherewithal to patrol the sector, millions of eyes look at nonprofit projects every day. The Guo Meimei/Red Cross incident became a scandal when her post of lavish spending went viral. So did a video of a rat at the buffet table of one of Malaysia's largest public hospitals. Needless to say, the kitchens there are much better maintained now! Everyone with a smart phone becomes an investigative journalist and whistleblower. This powerful trend can bring about better governance and oversight.

Technology even helps with impact. Many organizations use technology as an integral part of their offerings. In this book, we saw organizations as diverse as Akademi Berbagi in Indonesia and Tree Planet in South Korea use the Internet to communicate and as their distribution system. They also illustrate the circular aspect of using technology well. When an organization fundraises successfully online, it can then scale up its projects and report the increased impact, which assists in further fundraising and so on. We picked the 30 organizations in our studies because they were particularly successful. All of them spent time and resources developing their Internet presences, without which it would be more difficult to be successful today.

Another important recent trend in Asia drawing on relationships and technology is the wave of young people who see addressing social challenges as a viable career option. This is new. In the chapter on philanthropists, we cited the historical tendency for the best and the brightest to go into lucrative careers, a phenomenon contributing to the trust deficit hurdle of charitable organizations. Such narrow career choices made sense when Asia was just coming out of widespread poverty. Now, more and more young people want to work with SDOs, with philanthropic foundations, in social enterprises and impact investing. There is energy and enthusiasm for using business to achieve social good, and while these social enterprises have not made significant difference to date, it is still early days and many are moving into this sector. No doubt, scalable social innovations will proliferate and present us with solutions that haven't been available before.

Certain innovations skip past steps followed in the West. We can see how cell phone coverage, for example, arrived in Asia before the full distribution of land lines. With an incomplete network of telephone lines, mobile technologies were able to "leap-frog" to massive scale quite quickly. The dearth of landline infrastructure was not just about the hardware but the environment as well. While it is true that there were fewer phone lines in place, there were also fewer stakeholders with their own agendas to deal with. In the United States, the pre-existing phone companies put up road blocks to cell phones as they were slow to realize how critically important this technology was going to be. Similarly, in China, banks leapt past the use of paper checks. Once people became wealthy enough to substantially increase their regular purchases, transactions went digital to a degree surpassing the West. In 2016, mobile payments in China were 50 times those in America.

In the charitable sector, we find similar factors in place. Throughout Asia, human and organizational infrastructures are sparser and newer. This means that if we find better models, best practices, enabling regulations, and policies, they can be put in place now, allowing Asia to maximize the way that private social investment is made, and to apply it in ways that leverage it much more effectively. It is also true that without established agendas, we have an opportunity to really start with fresh ideas and innovative models.

To see what is possible in the charitable sector, we can look to the "green revolution," the widespread adoption of new seeds and agricultural processes in the 1960s that dramatically increased production worldwide, especially in developing countries, allowing millions to receive better food and nutrition. The green revolution succeeded through five complementary factors: application of new technology, an enabling environment (especially through improved fertilizer and irrigation), the training of an energized cohort of young people in new techniques, sufficient funding, and solid relationships with governments.

All these factors apply now to the charitable sector. In this case, the "technology" consists of the application of better models and best practices as well as the use of the Internet and mobile applications. The enabling environment comes through the popularity of engagement and "giving back" now becoming increasingly popular in Asia. This is important as it is much more organic, more natural. And although there was one unfortunate outcome of the green revolution with the deleterious environmental impact of the same fertilizers that dramatically and somewhat unnaturally increased yield, there is no doubt that much more good took place. The training of young people is also happening apace, at the university level through classes on nonprofit management, philanthropy, corporate social responsibility, and through incubators and hubs for social enterprises. Governments have set up funds for the creation of social enterprises and for other types of social projects, including trainings, workshops, and mentoring of those who receive the funds. On the funding side, while the numbers are difficult to pin down exactly, there is ample evidence of a fast-growing philanthropic movement in Asia.

Which brings us to the last factor: solid relationships with government. As we have discussed throughout this book, this is an area where Asia differs dramatically from the West. There is a social contract in place in Asia. Donors tend to fund projects, programs, and social needs that are aligned with the government's goals in their country, and many successful SDOs do the same. This is true throughout the region. Sometimes this cooperation is explicit. For example, in China, where the new charity law limits the work of SDOs to poverty relief, care for the elderly and orphans, disaster relief, education, science, culture, and sports—all issues the government has prioritized for itself as well. In most cases, the understanding is implicit. There is some degree of self-policing in which donors choose to fund programs that comply with government priorities without being told to do so.

There are ramifications in having this social contract. One important one is that when government is involved with an effort to address a social challenge, the idea or innovation can be picked up by the government and scaled in a way that would have been impossible if only the SDO were administering it. *Scale* is a term that receives much fanfare in the social investment community today. Scale and systemic change are not the same thing. Scale means significantly increasing the number of products or services. *Systemic change* refers to addressing the causes of the problem and changing the system so that it does not occur again or at least with the same frequency. To achieve great scale and carry out systemic change, you need the government to be involved. The good news in Asia is that in most cases, the government is already involved. What does not happen often enough is that the government is nimble or honest enough to see a solution and then change direction to accommodate it. It is for this reason that some philanthropists, such as the Azim Premji Foundation and Tata Trusts in India, and Wash SyCip and the Jon Ramon Aboitiz Foundation in the Philippines, have begun to train government officials on how to be better at their jobs so that they can more readily put in place viable solutions.

Another benefit of the social contract is the degree to which it brings about societal harmony within a country. Harmony is a prized value and outcome in the region. It is integral to the "Asian way" prescribed by Prime Ministers Mahathir and Lee Kuan Yew. It is also a way to mitigate critique and maintain social cohesion. The new laws in India, China, and Indonesia seem to push in this direction. In a much-cited article, Harvard University professors Roberto Foa and Yascha Mounk argue that based on public opinion polling, young people, especially those in developed countries, are not satisfied with their governments and are open to alternatives, including benevolent authoritarian regimes.[3]

In Asia, most have not known any other kind of governance. We are at a pivotal juncture. It is possible that with more government curbs on nonprofits engaging in advocacy—combined with the trend labeled in this book as "DIY philanthropy," when companies take on addressing social challenges on their own and do not work with and through nonprofit organizations—those organizations will starve. We could witness the withering away of those parts of civil society acting as contrarian voices, while at the same time improving the social indicators and certain aspects of the quality of life for many.

On the other hand, with other new trends—including use of the Internet and social media, and the outpouring of support to address social challenges from the region's youth—we could see an activation of civil engagement unparalleled in Asian history.

Throughout Asia, the seesaw dynamism between old and new influences societal evolution in new and interesting ways. There is considerable variation across the region, but the presumption that every country would take on the attributes of the developed Western world has been debunked. Asia is evolving with unique characteristics that differentiate it from the West.

In Chapter 1, we proposed to answer the following questions:

- Is there an "Asian" way of doing good? If there is, why so, and what are the implications?
- What is the Asian philanthropy and social delivery ecosystem, and how has it evolved?
- What are the characteristics and strategies of successful Asian SDOs?
- Why is it important to distinguish between SDOs and other types of nonprofit organizations?
- What are trends of Asian philanthropists and why?
- What are shared challenges for the region?
- What can donors, SDO policymakers, and the public at large do to enable the social sector to thrive and contribute to improving the lives of people throughout the region?

Only the last has not been sufficiently answered. In order to do so, we must ask ourselves fundamental questions about the world we want to live in and what values are important to us. Many say that we are living in the Asian century. Time will tell what the implications of that truly are.

Asia has grown into the most dynamic economic region in the world today. Change is happening with great dispatch. Until recently, there has not been much infrastructure around the charitable sector, a condition improving rapidly along with the expanding reach of philanthropic efforts. These charitable aims grow through long-standing traditions, including the importance of relationships and an interest in family, as well as through newer developments, like the leveraging of technology and governmental partnerships. While the region retains its challenges, many will be met through the increased means and desire for doing good.

Notes

1. Kemp, Simon. "Digital in 2016: Data, Trends and Insights." Tech in Asia. February 22, 2016. https://www.techinasia.com/talk/digital-2016-data-trends-insights. Accessed July 30, 2017.
2. Global Internet Report 2016. The Internet Society. http://www.internetworldstats.com/top20.htm. Accessed July 30, 2017.
3. Foa, Roberto Stephan and Yascha Mounk. "The Danger of Deconsolidation: The Democratic Disconnect." *Journal of Democracy*, 27.3 (July 2016).

Selected Bibliography

Cagney, Penelope, and Bernard Ross, eds. *Global Fundraising: How the World Is Changing the Rules of Philanthropy*. John Wiley & Sons, Inc., 2013.

Callahan, David. *The Givers: Wealth, Power, and Philanthropy in a New Gilded Age*. Alfred A. Knopf, 2017.

Cheng, Willie, and Sharifah Mohamed, eds. *The World that Changes the World: How Philanthropy, Innovation, and Entrepreneurship Are Transforming the Social Ecosystem*. Jossey-Bass, 2010.

Cheng, Willie. *Doing Good Well: What Does (and Does Not) Make Sense in the Nonprofit World*. Epigram Books, 2015.

Cheng, Willie, et al. *Doing Good Great: Thirteen Asian Heroes and Their Causes*. Epigram Books, 2015.

Friedman, Lawrence J., and Mark D. McGarvie, eds. *Charity, Philanthropy, and Civility in American History*. Cambridge University Press, 2002.

Gillis, E. Kay. *Singapore Civil Society and British Power*. Talisman Publishing Company, Singapore. 2005.

Hasan, Samuil, and Jenny Onyx, eds. *Comparative Third Sector Governance in Asia*. Springer Press, New York, NY, 2008.

Huang, Chien-Chung, Guosheng Duo, Zhenyao Wang, and Richard Edwards, eds. *China's Nonprofit Sector: Progress and Challenges*. Transaction Publishers, New Brunswick, NJ, 2014.

Ilchman, Warren F., et al., eds. *Philanthropy in the World's Traditions*. Indiana University Press, 1998

Osborne, Stephen P., ed. *The Voluntary and Non-Profit Sector in Japan: The Challenge of Change*. RoutledgeCurzon, 2003.

Salamon, Lester M., et al. *Global Civil Society: Dimensions of the Nonprofit Sector*. Vol. 1, The Johns Hopkins University, 1999.

R.A. Shapiro et al., *Pragmatic Philanthropy*,
https://doi.org/10.1007/978-981-10-7119-5

Salamon, Lester M., S. Wojciech Sokolowski, et al. *Global Civil Society: Dimensions of the Nonprofit Sector*. Vol. 2, Kumarian Press, 2014.

Simon, Karla W. *Civil Society in China: The Legal Framework from Ancient Times to the "New Reform Era"*. Oxford University Press, 2013.

Tsu, Yu Yue. *The Spirit of Chinese Philanthropy; A Study in Mutual Aid*. HardPress Publishing, 2013.

Wiepking, Pamala, and Femida Handy, eds. *The Palgrave Handbook of Global Philanthropy*. Palgrave Macmillan, 2015.

Witt, Michael A., and Gordon Redding, eds. *The Oxford Handbook of Asian Business Systems*. Oxford University Press, 2015.

Index[1]

[1] Note: Page numbers followed by 'n' refers to notes.

R.A. Shapiro et al., *Pragmatic Philanthropy*,
https://doi.org/10.1007/978-981-10-7119-5

PGMO 04/20/2018